WHAT ABOUT ME?

WOMEN AND THE CATHOLIC CHURCH

SHARON TIGHE-MOONEY

FOREWORD BY MARY T. MALONE

MERCIER PRESS

IRISH PUBLISHER – IRISH STORY

MERCIER PRESS

Cork

www.mercierpress.ie

© Text: Sharon Tighe-Mooney, 2018
© Foreword: Mary T. Malone, 2018

ISBN: 978 1 78117 540 8

10 9 8 7 6 5 4 3 2 1

A CIP record for this title is available from the British Library

Printed and bound in the EU.

I'd rather live my life as if there is a God

and die to find out there isn't,

than live my life as if there isn't

and die to find out there is.

Attributed to the French philosopher
Albert Camus (1913–60)

For Liam and Luke,
with love and gratitude.

CONTENTS

THE MAJOR ERAS OF CHRISTIANITY

1st–2nd century	New Testament times
2nd–6th century	Hellenistic, Patristic model
3rd–4th century	Medieval Latin Catholic model (finalised 11th–15th century)
16th century	Protestant Reformation model
17th–19th century	Enlightenment model
20th–21st century	Postmodern, Ecumenical model[1]

FOREWORD

What I liked immediately about this book was its straightforward, clear and explicit title: *What About Me? Women and the Catholic Church.* The question of women haunts the Catholic Church and has done so for centuries, but, despite mountains of papal encyclicals, the Church is no closer to peaceful co-existence with women.

It was Bernard Lonergan, the great Canadian Jesuit theologian, who suggested that the most radical thing a person could do was to name the obvious. This is what this book sets out to do without excuse or prevarication, and the author, Sharon Tighe-Mooney, delivers to a superlative degree what she promises. The Catholic Church is entirely male dominant in its leaders, its teachers, its hierarchical clergy structure, its liturgy, its language and its exclusively male-metaphored God. We women are so accustomed to it that we barely notice it and we continue the daily task of claiming our personhood and naming our God in the most toxic of circumstances.

It is noticeable that in the past few years the Catholic Church itself has officially ceased to attempt an explanation of this situation and has retreated to the least convincing position, that of proclaiming its authority to decide such issues. The most recent such proclamation came from Pope Francis, who, when queried about the priestly ordination of women, replied, 'that door is closed'.

Attempts at a theological explanation of the status of women as nonentities in the Catholic Church go back centuries, but a series of recent statements continues to attempt such an explanation. In 1943 Pope Pius XII suggested that women and men were 'absolutely equal' *coram deo*, in the sight of God, but in the sight of men, however, this was not the case as women and men had been assigned specific roles in the 'order of creation' and women would always be in a position of subordination to men. In the 1970s Paul VI brought further confusion to the issue. On the one hand he made Teresa of Ávila and Catherine of Siena Doctors of the Church, thus contradicting the apostle Paul's dictum that women could not teach in the Church. On the other hand, he issued what became the definitive statement against the ordination of women, *Inter Insigniores*. This document was greeted so negatively by theologians worldwide that it struck a blow at further attempts at theological explanations about why women had to occupy an inferior status in the Church.

Pope John Paul II contributed two more definitive statements to the subject. They were 'ontological complementarity' and the 'genius of femininity'. Each of these deals with the fundamentally auxiliary position of women in the Catholic Church, and bring us to the nub of the issue. In one sense, the question of ordination has been a good distraction for the Catholic Church. It has drawn attention away from the essence of the issue about women, and that is femaleness, the full female humanity and personhood of women.

For the Catholic Church femaleness is at the opposite pole to divinity. The Church is happy to talk about femininity, the 'nice' cultural attributes of women. It can even speak of femininity in God who is kind and merciful and displays other womanly secondary attributes. But femaleness is another matter.

What a relief then to turn to the writings of Christian women, specifically the medieval women mystics, who proclaimed with absolute confidence, 'My real me is God' and who celebrated their relationship of intimacy and even identity with God. At one of the most misogynistic periods in the history of Christianity, these women found their own appropriate way of speaking to and of God. And this fundamentally is the meaning of mysticism, which has been the woman's way of bypassing male mediation and naming and claiming their own God.

There are two kinds of Christians, two kinds of Catholics, women Catholics and men Catholics. The story of male Christianity has been the absolutely predominant version of Christianity and Catholicism available to us. Now, thanks to women such as Sharon Tighe-Mooney, we are beginning to hear the women's story of Christianity, of Catholicism and, even more importantly, of God.

Mary T. Malone
Wexford, 2018

INTRODUCTION

I was rather taken aback by the Vatican's 2010 decision, under the papacy of Benedict XVI (2005–13), to upgrade the 'sin' of ordaining a woman. Considering the context at the time – with worldwide revelations about the child abuse scandal, the vast scale of cover-up and secrecy, and the hostile stance taken towards victims – this was, to my mind, a rather strange move. In addition, given that women are forbidden from ministry in the Catholic Church, as well as being personally unaware of any specific public call for the ordination of women, I was puzzled by the timing and curious about what the move actually meant for women. First and foremost, it suggested that the Church meant business on this issue. There was to be no more discussion, and all pertinent people, such as seminarians, ordinands, clergy and theologians in Catholic institutions, are now obliged to take an oath affirming this position, among others, on Church teachings.

To close down all avenues of discussion, as John Paul II (1978–2005) had similarly done, seemed a defensive action. For me, it prompted the question of what it was that the men of the Church feared. Why make something that was already sinful and forbidden a more serious 'sin'? I was also curious to see what it said about the Church's attitude to women. Why at that time? What was the motivation, and more important, what were the implications?

I should point out that I felt seriously offended by this action. I have never understood why, as the Church teaches, the Holy Spirit would not call women to serve as ordained ministers when clearly women are and always have been called to serve God: within the restrictions placed upon them by the men of the Church, that is. I should also point out that while many women feel the same as I do about this, many other women do not. In other words, just as is the case for men, *all* women do not think and feel the same way about everything. Just as with men, they have different opinions, experiences and motivations. This is something I think needs to be said because, when reading material issued by the institutional Church, I have been struck by the recurring perspective on women, which is, first, that the value of women is completely bound up with their role as mothers; and second, the assumption that all women are the same.

I realised that I wanted to explore the story of women in the Christian movement and find the origin of such strongly held negative views about women. The Catholic Church is influential in many parts of the world. Many women live their lives according to its edicts while being denied access to its organisational ranks. In my view, while gender inequality continues to exist in organised religions, the barrier to full participation for women in all aspects of society will continue. This might seem like a weighty claim, but if we look at the aspirational aspects of many religions, which encourage people to respect and value one another, the secondary position of women in these religious structures undermines that message. Moreover, the scriptures have been used again and again to position women as inferior beings. In other words, we are supposed not only to believe, but also to accept, that while humans are equal in the eyes of God, this does not mean that women have equal access to priestly ministry. So the teaching that we are all one in Christ Jesus has restrictions. In my view, while this dichotomous worldview persists, violence against or abuse of anyone perceived as 'other', in this case, women, is implicitly condoned.

My own background is Catholic and I am a long-time member of a church choir. I believe in God and in the survival of the soul or spirit after death. I do not believe that God is sexist, racist or homophobic. Nor do I believe that one faith system is necessarily 'better' than another. I have at times found church rituals to be somewhat comforting or soothing. I have heard wonderfully affirming words and ideas expressed from the altar to help people cope with life, its trials and its tribulations. At the same time, I have also been seriously irritated and offended at the views delivered from the pulpit. In my case, the idea of a group of mostly elderly white men imposing their views and their will on women's lives and decisions, without any consultation or even regard for women, gradually began to rankle. How had it come to pass that our lives could be shaped and formulated by celibate men living in an autonomous enclave in Rome? Furthermore, what kind of God would divinely ordain the superiority and authority of one Christian over another?

My journey towards questioning the tenets of Catholicism began as a series of unrelated events. Many will recall collections for 'black babies' from their schooldays. We were told that these babies were doomed to spend eternity in Limbo unless saved by missionaries. I was stunned by this revelation. How could innocent babies, because of where they happened to be born, be subject to such a fate? I simply could not accept this as being true. Questioning such edicts, however, was simply not done at the time, as my experience of Church teaching in convent school and in the Church itself was one based on the notion of sin and guilt, on the imposition of rules and with the expectation of unquestioning obedience. As a result, I felt as an adult that I knew very little about Catholicism and its history. Sharing a house with Protestant and Presbyterian friends many years later made it clear to me how little I knew about my faith in contrast to my housemates' impressive knowledge of theirs.

As the years went by, I found myself continuously irritated at having to deal with everything from a male point of view. I also had difficulty with the diametrically opposed edict of, on the one hand, placing responsibility for the perpetuation of the faith on Catholic women, and, on the other, the complete exclusion of women's voices in decision-making in the Church. Where, as a woman, was I supposed to fit in? How, as a woman, was I supposed to identify with such a male-centred Church? Moreover, how can a Church that is identified as a loving Church be so disdainful about half its membership because of their gender?

Some years later I happened to be studying the fiction of the Irish writer Kate O'Brien (1897–1974) for my doctorate, and what really interested me was her exploration of the impact that Catholic Church edicts had on the way her female characters thought, behaved and conducted their lives. During my research, I came across a copy of Mary McAleese's *Reconciled Being: Love in Chaos*. In her book,

McAleese mentions that while she was writing a speech to be delivered in a church the following day, it occurred to her that she was probably the first woman to stand in the pulpit without a tin of polish and a duster in her hand! The image stuck in my mind and I began to question the extent of the role that the Catholic Church had played in the experiences and lives of women. This, in turn, led me into an exploration of the representation of women in the Bible and in Christian writings. To a large extent, the motive for writing this book was to find out what I wanted to know myself.

The many questions I had about women's lack of place in the Roman Catholic Church ultimately boiled down to two: first, why do Catholic women not have a role in the organisational model of their own Church? And second, why is the institutional Church so opposed to the idea of female ministry that the Vatican is prepared to dismiss, excommunicate and censure their own personnel for attempting to discuss the topic? In the quest for knowledge and enlightenment, I have been helped greatly by the many excellent books published on the subject by historians and theologians, whose work has contributed to and assisted this personal exploration immensely. The research I have drawn from most especially includes *Women and Christianity*, in three volumes, by Mary T. Malone; *The Gospel According to Woman* by Karen Armstrong; *Eunuchs for Heaven* by Uta Ranke-Heinemann; and *The Ordination of Women in the Catholic Church* by John Wijngaards. Mary T. Malone is a former Professor of Theology at the Toronto School of Theology, now living in Ireland. Karen Armstrong is a former religious sister and has written many books on faith and the major religions. Uta

Ranke-Heinemann is a convert to Catholicism and the daughter of the former President of West Germany, Gustav Heinemann (1969–74). She was a classmate of Pope Benedict XVI's at the University of Munich in the early 1950s. In 1970 she became the first woman in the world to hold a chair of Catholic theology at the University of Essen, which she lost in 1987, however, after denying the Virgin Birth. She has been one of the most outspoken critics of Pope John Paul II. John Wijngaards is a former Vicar General of the Mill Hill Missionaries and founder of the Wijngaards Institute for Catholic Research, based in England. In 1998 he resigned from his priestly ministry in protest against Pope John Paul II's decrees *Ordinatio Sacerdotalis* and *Ad Tuendam Fidem*, which forbade further discussion about the topic of women priests in the Catholic Church.

A word about how sources have been noted might be useful. A frequently used source is the *Catechism of the Catholic Church*. The *Catechism* was commissioned by the Council of Trent (1545–63) and published in 1566 for use by priests. It was reissued by Pope John Paul II in 1994, and this is the edition used throughout. In the introductory letter of the *Catechism*, Pope John Paul II described the work as 'a statement of the Church's faith and of catholic doctrine, attested to or illumined by Sacred Scripture, the Apostolic Tradition and the Church's Magisterium'.[1] In other words, the statements or teachings are, he said, supported by the Bible, the apostles, their successors and the Magisterium or teaching authority of the Church. All paragraphs in the *Catechism* are numbered, and so the usual manner of referencing is used, which is to cite the particular paragraph referred to rather than the page number. All Bible references are taken from *The HarperCollins Study Bible*, unless otherwise stated. Quotations are referenced in endnotes and all sources are listed in the bibliography by author surname in alphabetical order.

Ancient sources are a little different. The individual gospels are first divided into chapters and then into sections or verses. A quotation from the Gospel of Mark in the Bible will therefore look like this: (Mark 2.14), that is, the Gospel of Mark, chapter two, verse fourteen; and Mark 2.14–16 is the Gospel of Mark, chapter two, verses fourteen to sixteen. In addition, for reasons of brevity, the various gospels, such as the Gospel of Mark, for example, are on occasion referred to as 'Mark' or 'Mark's gospel'. Similarly, the term, 'Church', will be used hereafter to refer to the Roman Catholic Institutional Church Organisation. Dates following the names of popes and archbishops relate to their years in office; other dates following individuals' names relate to birth and death years.

I am conscious that the subject matter is an area of deep personal significance to many people. Moreover, there is little doubt about the importance of faith in the lives of millions of people around the world. While many may not agree with what I have to say, the aim of this book is not to convince, but rather to discuss. Like most things in life, there are no simple, clear-cut answers. Rather, what I offer here is one perspective, based on the research undertaken to find some answers to my questions; questions that many historians and theologians have also posed and investigated. What interests me is how those questions have been answered by the

Vatican, and how such answers resonate with an ordinary lay person, such as myself, reading the material for themselves. My hope is that readers will find my discoveries interesting and thought-provoking.

1

THE EARLY CHRISTIAN MOVEMENT

HOW THE GOSPELS CAME ABOUT

Whether we are aware of it or not, the way we think and behave in the West has been framed by a Christian heritage. That heritage includes a specific worldview of women's 'nature' and role in society. While there have been important cultural advances for women in this regard, the one institution that has not altered its perception of women to any great degree is the Roman Catholic Church. The Bible, as well as Christian texts and history, were written by men, about men and for a male audience. Moreover, these works have been interpreted and taught by men. Thus women are presented from a male perspective. Of course, women are and always have been present in all aspects of societal, cultural and religious development, but their thoughts, opinions and actions are not recorded in the same way as those of men. As a result, it can be difficult to 'read' their story, a position of which the teaching authority of the Church has taken advantage, despite the proliferation of scholarly work since the 1960s addressing this discrepancy.

The Church argues that they follow the example of Jesus, who chose men for his apostolic team, to maintain a male-only ministry. Evidence to support this teaching is gleaned from the scriptures, particularly the New Testament, wherein the life, teachings, death and resurrection of Jesus are recorded. Thus, because the scriptures are used by the teaching authority of the Catholic Church to position women as secondary and to exclude them from ministry in the Catholic Church, we need to know something about the origins of the Gospels and the other books in the New Testament to understand the position it takes.[1] The difficulty with what is recorded in the New Testament is that Jesus himself did not write anything down, and neither did his immediate group of followers. His words were passed on by word of mouth. While oral traditions preserve key features, they are liable to suffer amendments, additions, omissions and rewordings, and as a result, are essentially fluid.

It was at least twenty years after Jesus' death before any written evidence about him was composed. When accounts of him were eventually written, they were aimed at a range of audiences, written to address contemporary issues and consequently moulded to fit particular circumstances.

The earliest written accounts we have are the letters of St Paul (c. AD 10–62), the most prominent missionary of the early Church and a convert to the Christian movement following his vision on the road to Damascus. These letters are, to a large extent, answers to questions posed by the communities Paul had established, about the young, burgeoning faith and how to practise it. It is important to bear in mind that the early movement, which could be described as a splinter group from Judaism, meant that the boundary between Christian and Jew remained indistinct for quite some time.

The long period of time, perhaps as much as a hundred

years, over which the accounts of Jesus were written down, explains the various anomalies we shall see between accounts of events in the four gospels and Acts of the Apostles. Moreover, written material discovered in two caches in the twentieth century suggest that diversity of religious belief and practice was a feature of the early Christian movement as it sought to establish itself.

In 1945 a large hoard of written material from the early centuries of the Christian movement was discovered in a jar in Egypt. Some fifty-two texts survive, including gospels, prayers and secret books of wisdom. They have been dated to around AD 350–400 and drew on material from, it is argued, the first to third centuries. These are known as the Gnostic Gospels or the Nag Hammadi Codices, the latter name relating to where they were discovered. These texts, on the one hand, emphasised salvation through secret knowledge, and on the other, contained similar as well as contrasting ideas and debates about Jesus, scripture and salvation to that found in the Gospels. For example, one sect, the Gnostics, argued that it was the knowledge (*gnosis*) of Jesus' message, rather than his death and crucifixion, that saved humanity. However, they believed that this secret knowledge was revealed to only a few.

The second discovery was the Dead Sea Scrolls, found in a number of caves along the west bank of the Dead Sea and the River Jordan, between 1946/7 and 1956. These have a much earlier provenance – *c.* 250 BC to AD 100 – and contain elements of the Hebrew Scriptures, commentary on the Old Testament and accounts of daily life in a Jewish community. According to Mark Humphries in *Early Christianity* this material also includes stories about a number of people claiming messianic status.[2]

These two discoveries indicate that a myriad of sources about Jesus and other religious-type figures, such as prophets and teachers, were in circulation up to at least the fourth century. These sources, coupled with the concern for 'false teachers' that St Paul writes about in his letters, suggest that Jesus' status as Messiah had to be fought for. As a result, the question of deciding which written records were 'authentic' accounts of Jesus' life and teachings was an inevitable step in the attempt to establish some form of unity in the burgeoning Christian movement. In *The Gnostic Gospels*, Elaine Pagels relates that Bishop Irenaeus of Lyons (178–200) 'insisted that all churches throughout the world must agree on all vital points of doctrine'.[3] Thus, Pagels explains, texts that did not share the same point of view as that decided upon by the Church were to be excluded; in other words, deemed heretical. The chosen works, it was decided, should represent certain truths that were thought to be inspired by God through the Holy Spirit.

The gradual compilation of the definitive list of books to be accepted by all Christians took over 300 years of protracted discussion. Eventually, uniformity of doctrine, ritual, canon (from the ancient Greek word for a rule or measure) and structure was established. In this way, scattered Christian groups gradually became more unified or catholic (which means universal) as accepted interpretations, doctrines and rituals were implemented.

As a result of this process, many written accounts of Jesus' life, work and death, and accounts attributed to some apostles and disciples, were excluded from the canon. The omitted material includes gospels attributed to Mary Magdalene, Thomas, Philip and James, though some of these were included in the New Testament in some churches for a time. Additionally, there were texts, Pagels writes, that questioned whether all suffering, labour and death derive from human sin, or whether Christ's resurrection should be taken as symbolic rather than literal. Others celebrated the divine feminine as well as masculine. Some had Jesus speak of illusion and enlightenment rather than of sin and repentance, while others depicted him as not being distinct from humanity, but with the self and the divine as being identical. The implication was that to know God is to be, or to share in, the divine. In addition, some intimated that Jesus had come as a guide and facilitator for spiritual understanding, and not to save us from sin.

In any case, by the end of the fourth century AD twenty-seven texts from the myriad of written material available had been collated as the official New Testament canon. These are: the gospels of Matthew, Mark, Luke and John (the word gospel comes from the Greek word for good news or message); twenty-one letters; the Revelation of John, which is a catastrophic vision of the future; and Acts of the Apostles, an account of the deeds of Jesus' immediate successors. Thus the written Christian tradition is a selection of texts chosen from a range of material that presented various accounts, as well as interpretations, of the life, death and teachings of Jesus.

As a result of the range of available sources, there are anomalies in the four gospel accounts. For example, the descriptions of Jesus' origins vary from account to account. We know that he was born during the reign of King Herod, who died in 4 BC, and that he was crucified at some time between AD 26 and 29. Nothing is known about his childhood and early manhood, and the story of the census obliging the family to travel to Bethlehem at the time of his birth is recounted only in the Gospel of Luke. Mark describes Jesus as a carpenter: 'Is not this the carpenter, the son of Mary and brother of James and Joses and Judas and Simon, and are not his sisters here with us?' (Mark 6.1–4). However, Matthew describes him as the son of a carpenter: 'Is not this the carpenter's son? Is not his mother called Mary? And are not his brothers James and Joseph and Simon and Judas? And are not all his sisters with us?' (Matthew 13.55–56). Whatever his occupation, it seems clear that Jesus was part of a large family, a fact to bear in mind later when discussing Our Lady.

The notion of Jesus' three-year ministry is based on the Gospel of John, as his account mentions three Passovers (John 2.13; 6.3; 19.31). According to the other gospels, however, his ministry could have been as short as one year. The reasons for his arrest also vary among the accounts, although all agree that the resurrection happened on the third day. In addition, the sequence of events is different from one gospel to the next.

The reasons for such variations arise from the circumstances in which the four gospels were written: from the sources the authors used and the cultural context of the times. Matthew's and Luke's accounts are based on Mark's gospel, with all three appearing to share similar sources. As a result, they are called the synoptic gospels, from the Greek word, *synoptikos*, which means 'from the same point of view'. John's gospel is a later work that scholars argue could have been composed as much as fifty years after Mark's account. Most scholars agree that the Gospel of Mark was written first, though this is still debated. While the gospel is attributed to 'Mark', the author is unknown and it is thought to have been written between AD 69 and AD 75, some forty years after the death of Jesus, and long after the time of the apostles.

In *From Jesus to Christianity*, L. Michael White describes the background to the four accounts. Mark's gospel suggests an audience with a strong Jewish identity and the context of the gospel was the wiping out of the Jewish revolt against Roman rule and the destruction of their Temple. The Jews believed that after this suffering, and according to prophecies in Jewish scriptures, Christ would return to deliver them from their enemies. Their disappointment at this proving not to be the case, coupled with the successful suppression of the revolt by the Romans, seriously eroded their faith. They began to question whether Jesus really was the Messiah. The Gospel of Mark is a response to that uncertainty, as the author seeks to reassure his audience. To do so, he has to reappraise the belief in Christ's return in the light of what has occurred. As a result, the focus in this account is on the portrayal of a human, suffering Jesus, rather than a being of power, so as to align the story with the contemporary situation of his followers.

The next gospel, the Gospel of Matthew, written in Greek, is attributed to Matthew (or Levi), a tax collector and disciple of Jesus, but again, the actual author is unknown. It was not unusual at the time to attribute a work to an authoritative or well-known figure, to lend the work authenticity and gravitas. Matthew's gospel is thought to have been written around AD 80–90 and is also concerned with the role of the Jews in the new Christian movement, though Christian elements are more apparent here than in Mark's account. The focus in this text is on Jesus as a compassionate, healing Messiah. Also included are a number of instructions for living a good life and many warnings about the consequences of not doing so.

The Gospel of Luke and Acts of the Apostles are now thought to have been originally a single text. While they are attributed to Luke, the physician and travelling companion of St Paul, the author is unknown. The date of composition is debated, with a range from AD 90–100/110 likely, and the accounts appear to have been written for a Gentile rather than a Jewish audience, in contrast to the earlier gospels. Both works are dedicated to Theophilus, a name in Greek that is a combination of two words, meaning 'God' and 'love', and so this can be interpreted as being a dedication to those who love God. At the time dedicating a work was a common practice when writing the biography of an important person. There are new episodes introduced in Luke's gospel, such as the angel visiting Mary and the parables of the Prodigal Son and the Good Samaritan. Also evident is an emerging sense of self-definition as Christians, a term that was just beginning to be coined by Gentile followers of the Jesus movement. Luke's account, therefore, appears to be an attempt to flesh out the story of Jesus, while Acts describes the early days of establishing Christian communities, in particular Paul's role in that story.

In the final, or latest, account of Jesus, in the Gospel of John, the Jewish worldview is absent. In fact, there is a strong anti-Jewish rhetoric present, from where, it can be surmised, the anti-Jewish stance taken by the Church up to recent times emerged as being divinely sanctioned. In this account, the otherworldly or heavenly aspect of Jesus is premised, and he speaks in long monologues rather than parables. In addition, Jesus' humanity is downplayed, and there is much less of a focus on him as a suffering, crucified Messiah, or indeed on his life and work. Rather, his divinity is emphasised. Scholars believe that this gospel was composed during different periods and by different authors, with the last piece being written at any time between AD 95 and AD 120. The account appears to reflect the situation of an early Christian group attempting to break away from its Jewish origins and justifying that parting. Thus the intention of this account appears to be the encouragement of Christians in their growing sense of self-definition.

The gospels are, therefore, attempts to tell the story of Jesus for a particular audience in a particular context. We need to bear in mind that each writer had a particular purpose when writing their account of the life of Jesus. Additionally, there was a wide range of stories and materials to choose from when compiling these accounts. So, as the gospels were written anywhere between forty and ninety years after the death of Jesus, they are written reflections on his life, as well as expressions of faith, rather than accurate historical accounts.

'THE JESUS MOVEMENT'

The brief overview of the various gospels reflects what L. Michael White describes as 'the changing social location of the Jesus movement'.[4] In other words, there is initially a strong Jewish identity within the movement that grew up around Jesus and for quite some time after his death, that eventually moves away from that heritage towards a new self-defining one, that of Christian. Although, the 'Jesus movement' can be described as a sect originating within Judaism, Mark Humphries argues that the situation is more complex and 'that there is a problem with seeing Judaism as some sort of fixed religious system from which Christianity departed'.[5] Rather, the boundaries between Judaism and Christianity were indistinct as both were evolving belief systems; Christianity as a new religion and Judaism in the wake of the destruction of the temple in Jerusalem. Moreover, as White writes: 'Jesus did not come as the founder of a new religion, and yet a new religion, Christianity, was founded in his name or, more precisely, in his memory.'[6] This new religion, however, took many centuries to evolve.

While the idea of a straightforward, unbroken, unified system of belief from the time of Jesus was my experience of taught religion, the evolving development of the religious movement offers quite a different picture. As the gospels and St Paul's letters suggest, the early movement consisted of widely scattered groups with diverse cultural heritages, practising varying interpretations of Jesus' teachings and often situated in a hostile world. It is clear too from historical sources that the 'Jesus movement' was radical for its time, although any group that posed a threat to the occupying Roman army was at risk from prosecution. This is borne out by the sentence of crucifixion passed on its leader and the persecution of Jesus' followers, as well as accounts of the sporadic but persistent persecution of Christians in the early centuries of the movement. It was, therefore, a courageous act to become a follower of this new religion.

Given the complex historical context of the development of Christianity, it seems useful, at this point, to look more closely at the characteristics of the Jesus movement, in light of the Church's argument that the actions of Jesus, in relation to women, are explicit in terms of our exclusion from ministry. One radical aspect in the accounts of Jesus' life is his breaking of social barriers. The scriptures relate that he mingled with all sorts of people, regardless of race, position, occupation, gender or religious affiliation. In addition, interacting with women, and having women among his followers, was a significant statement for the time. Jesus' mission was to establish a new way of living, founded on the principles of love and forgiveness, with participation based on new ideas of unity and definition. He offered a new type of community, one that crossed the usual boundaries of race or place. In the introduction to *Writing in the Sand*, Thomas Moore writes: 'The point of Jesus' mission is not to draw attention to himself but to transform the way human beings live.'[7] Then, as now, it is people's way of thinking and dealing with others that he challenged. It was a challenge that, it can be argued, the modern world is still unable to embrace, as gender, sexuality, race and religion are categories still used by many organised religions, as well as various cultures, as barriers to inclusion.

In *The Ordination of Women in the Catholic Church*, John Wijngaards remarks that Jesus did not make a lot of decisions in general, or indeed, supply a handy list of detailed rules and regulations. That is why so much of faith and practice is based on interpretation. The Jewish Jesus did not condemn or abolish the Jewish faith or the Law of Moses: 'Do not think that I have come to abolish the law or the prophets; I have come not to abolish but to fulfil' (Matthew 5.17). Jesus did not formalise the groups of people, both men and women, who accompanied him. He did not establish a Church with structures such as we have today. He did not give us Canon Law, or reams of instructions on how to conduct rites or train religious personnel.[8] He did not explicitly institute sacraments such as marriage and confirmation. Nor did he ordain anyone. Thus Jesus did not anticipate every situation by issuing rules to be obeyed slavishly and unthinkingly. Rather, he expected people to apply the aspirations he gave them to all their doings. He asked them to 'love one another'. In addition, there was the simple request: 'gather together in my name'. If, indeed, only the actions or words of Jesus were considered pertinent, we would be left with very little in terms of laws, rituals and sacraments in current Church practice. As Wijngaards remarks: 'In practically all matters of faith and practice, Jesus did not determine any of the details. What he did – and this was his crucial contribution – was to present ideals.'[9]

After the death of Jesus, this early Jewish/Christian movement was obliged to find its own path among the many variations of Jesus' teachings that were in circulation. Thus, discussion, questioning and reasoning was a marked feature of this new belief system. For example, in St Paul's letter to the Galatians, he demonstrates his concern for the churches of Galatia in Asia Minor, which are being challenged by unidentified teachers to observe elements of Jewish law and ritual. This reflects the central issue of debate in the early days of the movement as it evolved from its Jewish heritage to incorporate a wider membership. The admission of pagans or Gentiles, for example, was a contentious issue. Leaders such as Peter felt that Gentile converts should adopt certain Jewish practices such as circumcision. Paul disagreed but it appears that, at a meeting in Jerusalem, he failed to convince Peter to admit uncircumcised Gentiles to the Jesus movement. As a result, Paul decided to concentrate his mission on the conversion of Gentiles and went off around the Aegean by himself to do so. Thus there is a difference in practice between the groups led by Peter and Paul, even though they are both under the umbrella of the Jesus movement. What is of note, therefore, is that discussion, debate and difference of opinion was the hallmark of the evolving movement in a world of multiple belief systems.

The first Christian groups established by Paul were in modern-day Greece: first at Philippi, a Roman colony, and then Thessalonica, a Roman city by law, but with a Greek heritage and culture. Paul then travelled to Athens, and from there to Corinth. His letters to these communities both instruct and answer questions relating to faith and practice. They also reflect the difficulties of bringing together Jewish, Greek and Roman cultural and religious heritages under the new umbrella of Christianity.

Paul is anxious to assert that Jewish law has now been superseded by a new faith that dispenses with former barriers. In his letter to the Galatians, he writes: 'There is no longer Jew or Greek, there is no longer slave or free, there is no longer male and female; for all of you are one in Christ Jesus' (Galatians

3.28). It can be argued that 'male and female' would not be included as a distinction to be discarded if irrelevant to God's message. The Old Testament intimates that God is beyond gender, or comprises both: 'So God created humankind in his image, in the image of God he created them; male and female he created them' (Genesis 1.27). Similarly, in Paul's writing, he is clear about the eradication of former distinctions based on status, race or gender. For example, with regard to Jews and non-Jews, Paul explains in his letter to the Ephesians that 'the Gentiles have become fellow heirs, members of the same body, and sharers in the promise in Christ Jesus through the gospel' (Ephesians 3.6). The most important point of these famous words is that former marks of separation or difference are replaced by a new unity of faith. Also implicit is a new type of community and a new way of belonging that no longer relies on state or nationality.

From my examination of the Jesus and early Jewish/ Christian movements, there are some points of note. Jesus' vision for the future was one that saw all people involved in living and practising the ideals he laid out for them, regard-less of gender, sexuality or race. Moreover, his starting point was clear: all are equal in the sight of God; all are imbued with the Holy Spirit; we must love one another. These maxims, in my view, leave the way in which any person might want to give him/herself to God in ministry open to selection by the Holy Spirit. This is how St Paul began his ministry: he felt that he had been called to do so. Furthermore, as Paul reminded his community: 'To each is given the manifestation of the Spirit for the common good' (1 Corinthians 12.7). In other words, all humans are given spiritual attributes, women as well as men. To assume that a woman cannot be called because of her gender is, frankly, presumptuous, as it is difficult to imagine that the Holy Spirit is sexist!

One of the most important things Jesus said was that the kingdom of God is *within* us: 'The kingdom of God is not coming with things that can be observed; nor will they say, "Look, here it is!" or "There it is!" For, in fact, the kingdom of God is within you' (Luke 17.20–21). Jesus' words tell us that the divine is in all of us; gender, race, nationality and all other earthly categories of distinction are irrelevant. Furthermore, we are all one, or in other words, all connected to or part of God or Source or the Universe, or whatever term you might want to use. These words suggest that, as the kingdom of God is within us, we have direct access to God and are not in need of mediators.

The key features of the early movement was its evolutionary nature, as believers had to adapt to circumstances and to the world that surrounded them. This necessitated much discussion about the interpretation of Jesus' teachings and how to practise Christian rituals. Thus the beginnings of the Christian movement, and its development, were complex rather than straightforward, and there was much debate and discussion. As a result, practices that are taken for granted today were not all there from the beginning. Rather, they were enacted, invented, dropped, amended and reaffirmed over time, often as responses to confrontation, or in light of new interpretations of the scriptures, or for a myriad of reasons that a living Church necessarily encounters in an evolutionary world. Even this necessarily brief survey of the development of Christianity does not support the idea of a fixed set of beliefs and practices preserved by the apostles and handed on to their successors.

THE EARLY CHURCH

The early Christian communities, as we have seen, were scattered across a Roman world of considerable diversity, with differing views on beliefs and practice. Gatherings were held in private houses or house churches. Indeed, the Greek word, *ekklesia*, from which we derive the word 'church', originally meant an assembly or congregation of people rather than an actual building. The 'church' was the people. I should point out that terminology in general can be problematic as our concept of words, such as church, do not have the same connotations or meaning today as they did in antiquity. For my purposes here, therefore, the term Church will be used to refer to the development of the organisational aspect of Christianity. Also, for ease of terminology, the terms Christian and Christianity will be used in place of the Jesus and Jewish/Christian movements as this term of identification became more widespread as the movement developed.

The gospels, letters of Paul and the Gnostic texts suggest that not only did diverse forms of Christianity flourish up to the second century, but all claimed authenticity of one form or another. The difficulty was how to decide which of the myriad of gospels and texts were authentic. As mentioned earlier, the desire for uniformity had begun in the second century with prominent bishops, particularly Irenaeus of Lyons, attempting to take charge of the disparate Christian groups, thus bringing some measure of uniformity to Christian beliefs and practices. This was helped by the fact that from this period onwards, bishops were invested with power and authority in both Church and society. Establishing a hierarchy meant better communication channels between scattered groups of Christians. Also, there was a need for some form of physical structure, to cater for the growing number of believers.

At the same time, Christian values were very much at odds with both the religion and the cultural values of the Roman world. Tradition was a central principle upheld by Roman society, so while the Jewish religion was objectionable to many, it at least had an ancient heritage, which could secure it some measure of tolerance, however grudgingly conceded. Christianity, however, was a new religion. In addition, and like Judaism, it proclaimed one God, an alien concept for the Romans, who worshipped many gods. Moreover, Christian values were perceived as directly opposing some of the pillars of Roman society. For example, Christian views on equality, if enforced, would be a threat to an economy that depended on slavery, though it should be noted that in the event, when Christianity became the official religion of the Empire, slavery was not abolished.

Other radical features of early Christian teaching were the safeguards provided to women that were not otherwise available to them, either legally or culturally, at that time. The New Testament commanded that husbands should treat their wives with the same consideration and love that Christ manifested for his Church. In addition, adultery in men was seen as an equally serious wrong as adultery in women; another new concept for an ancient society. Furthermore, Jesus' teachings on the two becoming one in marriage implicitly granted equal status to both partners. This was anathema to a society in which women's lives were largely controlled by their father or husband.

However, in some cases, Christians took their cue from the society in which they lived. Roman culture was very much concerned with status. The twin facets of status were authority and obedience, and this perspective was Christianised to cement male authority over women, owner over slave, bishop over priest, and so on. This is despite Jesus' antipathy to assertions of authority: 'Whoever wants to be first must be last of all and servant of all' (Mark 9.35). Jesus' words contrast strongly with the actual development of the Church, which had, and continues to hold, implicit views about hierarchy, a legacy that stems from the organisational model of the Roman Empire.

Christianity, for the reasons listed above, was viewed as quite a radical religion. The new religion grew slowly in the first and second centuries, and while there was considerable growth in the third century, it was the support given by the Emperor Constantine (306–37) in the fourth century that contributed to its expansion throughout the Roman Empire, becoming the official religion in 380. The gradual adoption of Christianity throughout the Empire from the fourth century onwards marked the beginning of the process of establishing the Roman Catholic Church as a major political, social and religious institution.

Averil Cameron, in *The Later Roman Empire, AD 284–430*, explains that there are conflicting theories as to why Constantine supported what was at the time a minority religion. Eusebius of Caesarea, whose Church history 'turned into a glorification of Constantine', wrote that the emperor had a vision before the Battle of the Milvian Bridge, a clash that would cement his power as emperor, which convinced him that the God of the Christians was on his side and would help bring him victory.[10] On the other hand, Zosimus, a late-fifth-century or early-sixth-century pagan writer, wrote that Constantine realised that Christianity was the only religion that would offer him forgiveness for his many crimes; his wife and son, for example, had both died in mysterious circumstances. Whatever the reasons for Constantine's support of Christianity, and perhaps the influence of his Christian mother played a part, it is doubtful, as Cameron points out, that 'Christianity would have become the dominant religion without imperial support'.[11]

Constantine undertook the building of a series of churches, including St Peter's in Rome, which gave the new religion a visibility hitherto unavailable to Christians. With growth comes organisation, and accordingly, the Church became organised and run like the empire itself – along patriarchal, hierarchical lines. This process had begun in the second century with the hierarchical model of bishop, priest and deacon, but in the wake of a wider authoritarian reach, women, who had played a part in the ministry of the early Church, began to be excluded formally from Church ministries and decision-making. It was an erratic and unevenly imposed agenda that was authorised as a rule at a major Church meeting held at Laodicea in 352. Despite this, while there is no evidence that women had any formal roles from AD 200 onwards, the material discovered at Nag Hammadi in 1945 suggests that women continued to lead and to serve in some Christian groups until at least the fifth century, with some evidence that they were active into the ninth century in Germanic lands.

It was Constantine, rather than any bishop, who convened the first council of the Catholic Church, at Nicaea in 325. The background to his decision to call a council was to achieve harmony in the wake of serious disputes over various aspects of Christianity. For example, the most vocal movement, Arianism, disputed Jesus' divinity and indeed, the question of the nature of Jesus' divinity was debated up to the fifth century. Although Constantine was concerned with the civil unrest that such disputes could engender throughout the Empire rather than with religious edicts, he was responsible for enacting the decisions reached at the council. Many of the decisions made by the large gathering of bishops, as well as Constantine himself (though it is difficult to establish his exact input), set a precedent for how the Church would be run in the future. For example, a declaration and summary of the Christian faith, known as the Nicene Creed, and which declared Jesus' divinity, was decided upon. The council also decided to fix a date for Easter based on the deductions made by Christians, rather than relying on the Jewish calendar as had been the practice up to that point. Twenty new laws, or canons, were also introduced. One of these was the prohibition of women, except family members, from the houses of clerics, which suggests that the drive for a celibate clergy was already under way. We shall return to this topic later.

In one of the new canons, 'special authority' was bestowed on the Church leaders of Alexandria, Antioch and Rome (the division between East and West in the Church did not come until later). There is much ambiguity and dispute over the function of 'special authority', as the Roman Catholic Church draws on this edict to position the Bishop of

Rome as the antecedent of the papacy. Also significant is the law that introduced notions about the superiority of one Christian over another by introducing the precedence of bishops and presbyters (elders or priests) over deacons in receiving the Eucharist or Holy Communion. From this Council, therefore, the organisational structure emerged that saw bishops from all over the Empire agreeing on doctrinal decisions, with Church authority given to regional leaders or to Rome alone, depending on individual interpretations of the canon in question, as well as the establishment of a strict hierarchy within Christianity.

Another significant occurrence from this period was the translation of the 'authentic' scriptural texts from Greek to Latin (the Vulgate) by the Roman biblical theologian Jerome (c. 340–420), who undertook the task at the request of Pope Damasus I (366–84) in 382. While earlier attempts had been made to do this work, Jerome undertook a more concerted effort. He revised the text a number of times, and cut and amended it at will. He also separated the apocryphal books from the canonical list of authoritative writings. The Apocryphal/Deuterocanonical books are works placed between the Old and New Testaments that are accepted by Catholics as part of the canon but are not considered to be 'inspired' in the same way as the gospels. It is highly unlikely that Jerome's own, often misogynistic, views on women were suppressed when undertaking his translation of the Bible.

Once Christianity grew as an established religion, its tenets began to be compromised as the success of the spread of Christianity was based on the ruthless imposition of Roman laws and culture on conquered nations. Additionally, the legacy of the advancement of the Christian Roman Empire was a hierarchical, patriarchal society that possessed superlative administrative skills and was run on the basis of clear demarcations of authority. The Roman Catholic Church is still organised in this way. The radical nature of Jesus' teachings on equality were subsumed and to some degree negated, to suit the cultural ethos.

My investigations into the history of the early Christian movement clearly show that discussion, disagreement, debate and eventual consensus, was a marked feature of the emerging religion, and this will be seen in some detail when we look at the letters of St Paul later. If exact instructions about how to proceed had been set down by Jesus, there would have been no necessity for such debate. Because he did not do so, everything had to evolve, and the origins of Christianity and its written sources are therefore fluid and complex. As a result, the teachings and deeds attributed to Jesus in the gospels are subject to different perspectives and interpretations.

At the same time, Jesus stressed consistently, by word and deed, that all are equal in the eyes of God, as humans are all created in the image and likeness of God. The Church, however, disagrees, and argues that this is not strictly the case when it comes to women. Furthermore, the teaching Magisterium uses the scriptures to support that view. While various popes have focused on the major role women play in the family and in society, and on their value and worth, the Church structure itself contradicts what it teaches, as women are not integral to the running of the organisation in any formalised capacity. We shall now look in a little more detail at the arguments for women's exclusion.

2

NO WOMEN ALLOWED

THE CHOSEN ONES: TWELVE MALE APOSTLES

The Catholic Church teaches that, as a woman, I cannot be a priest. My question is, why not? The response is given in the *Catechism of the Catholic Church* (hereafter, *Catechism*):

> When Christ instituted the Twelve, 'he constituted [them] in the form of a college or permanent assembly, at the head of which he placed Peter, chosen from among them.' Just as 'by the Lord's institution, St Peter and the rest of the apostles constitute a single apostolic college, so in like fashion the Roman Pontiff, Peter's successor, and the bishops, the successors of the apostles, are related with and united to one another.'[1]

Thus the Church teaches that Jesus initiated a permanent model of the male-only priesthood by choosing twelve male apostles, positioning Simon Peter as leader after the resurrection, and the apostles in turn invested their successors with their particular authority as witnesses to the life, teachings, death and resurrection of Jesus. From this stems the reasons given as to why women cannot minister in the Church:

(1) The example from Scripture of Christ choosing his apostles from among men.

(2) The constant practice of the Church which has imitated Christ in only choosing men.

(3) The living teaching authority of the Church that holds that the exclusion of women from the priesthood is in accordance with God's plan for his Church.[2]

The first reason cites the scriptures, which are our template for Christian values, and is used as evidence to claim that Jesus deliberately chose males, thereby intentionally excluding females from his apostolic team. The second and third reasons are simply justifications used to support the first reason. In other words, reasons two and three simply state that the Church has always followed this particular interpretation of Jesus' actions in the scriptures in relation to the apostles and believes this stance to be the will of God. In my view, therefore, the first reason is the one to investigate, as justification for the exclusion of women from ministry is said to be drawn specifically from Jesus' actions in the scriptures.

The Church holds that Jesus did not make any woman a member of his apostolic team. The *Catechism* states: "'Only a baptized man (*vir*) validly receives sacred ordination." The Lord Jesus chose men (*viri*) to form the college of the twelve apostles, and the apostles did the same when they chose collaborators to succeed them in their ministry.'[3] There are three points here: Jesus chose twelve male apostles, he commissioned them, and they in turn chose and commissioned males to succeed them. Twelve men, chosen by Jesus, are considered to be the representatives of the unbroken tradition of apostolic succession. This is the basis for the exclusion of women from ministry.

However, as we shall see, it is not specified that twelve particular men are called by Jesus to follow him. Others were sent out to spread the good news, both before and after the resurrection, who are also described as apostles or disciples. They are not named specifically in terms of who they are or the roles they have, and it should be noted that specific leadership roles did not evolve until much later. The meaning of the term apostle is that of a messenger, while a disciple is a learner or pupil. In other words, from the beginning, while the identity of the twelve is largely uniform, it cannot be ascertained that they alone were given the specific role of apostle as it is understood today.

Simon Peter appears in all the gospel accounts and in Acts of the Apostles, as does, it should be noted, Mary Magdalene. So too do Andrew, James and John (sons of Zebedee), Philip, Thomas and Judas Iscariot. Bartholomew is cited in the synoptic gospels and Acts but does not appear in John's gospel. Similarly, Matthew and James (son of Alphaeus) do not appear in John but are named in the other gospels as well as in Acts. Nathanael appears only in John's account. Finally, we have Judas in Acts; Thaddaeus in two accounts; Jude and Simon the Cananaean in two accounts; and Simon the Zealot in two more. Neither of the Simons is named in John's gospel. The differences between the synoptic accounts and John's gospel can be attributed to the different dates of composition as well as different contexts. What is important to note for our purposes here is that the identity of the chosen twelve is not absolutely certain.

The synoptic gospel accounts of the choosing of the twelve, and the mission given to them by Jesus, are quite similar, though there are also some interesting variations. In Mark's account we are told: '[Jesus] went up the mountain and called to him those whom he wanted, and they came to him. And he appointed twelve, whom he also named apostles, to be with him, and to be sent out to proclaim the message, and to have authority to cast out demons' (Mark 3.13–15). Later, we are told that Jesus 'called the twelve and began to send them out two by two, and gave them authority over the unclean spirits' (Mark 6.7). The apostles carried out their mission: 'They cast out many demons, and anointed with oil many who were sick and cured them' (Mark 6.13). The gift of healing seems paramount here.

In Matthew's gospel, which is a sort of missionary discourse, the disciples are instructed that the way to follow Jesus is as a wandering preacher and healer: 'Then Jesus summoned his twelve disciples and gave them authority over unclean spirits, to cast them out, and to cure every disease and every sickness' (Matthew 10.1). Jesus tells them: 'As you go, proclaim the good news, "The kingdom of heaven has come near"' (Matthew 10.7). Again, the disciples or apostles are given the gift of healing.

In the Gospel of Luke we are told that Jesus chooses twelve from the many disciples that are with him and calls them apostles (Luke 6.13). In this account, as in Matthew's gospel (see Matthew 28.16–20), the sending out or mission scene takes place later: 'Then Jesus called the twelve together and gave them power and authority over all demons and to cure diseases, and he sent them out to proclaim the kingdom of God and to heal' (Luke 9.1–2). However, in Luke's gospel, more disciples are sent out as missionaries: 'After this the Lord appointed seventy others and sent them on ahead of him in pairs to every town and place where he himself intended to go' (Luke 10.1). So, while the mission given by Jesus to the apostles or disciples is once again to proclaim the good news and to heal, in Luke's account many others, as well as the twelve, are also given this mission.

In John's gospel, the choosing of the twelve is not recorded specifically. Also, in this account, Simon Peter's brother, Andrew, encounters Jesus first. Andrew brings his brother to meet Jesus, who on seeing him says: '"You are Simon son of John. You are to be called Cephas" (which is translated Peter)' (John 1.42). The next day, Jesus asks Philip to follow him, and he in turn encourages Nathanael to join them (John 1.43–51). Nathanael does not appear in any of the other gospels. In addition, this particular gospel implies that some of the disciples were the disciples of John the Baptist. The fact that there are twelve is not mentioned until later (see, for example, John 6.67). Moreover, in this account, the apostles' mission is not specified directly using the same terms as in the synoptic gospels. For example, in an exhortation to his disciples or apostles that shares a similarity with the instructions given in Matthew (10.40), Jesus tells them: 'Very truly, I tell you, whoever receives one whom I send receives me; and whoever receives me receives him who sent me' (John 13.20). Later, when Jesus prays to his Father for his disciples just before his arrest, he says: 'As you have sent me into the world, so I have sent them into the world' (John 17.18). Neither remark specifies that the 'sending out' is confined to specific people; rather, *The HarperCollins Study Bible* explains, it is extended to the Church beyond them. It appears, therefore, that Jesus sent out many people to spread the good news, and that this role was not confined to the twelve apostles alone.

In terms of the specific priestly role given to twelve men, the Last Supper is perceived of as the scene wherein Jesus established bread and wine as a memorial of the sacrifice of his body and blood, and instituted the perpetual celebration of this sacrifice that could only be conducted by a male priest. At the Supper, we are told, Jesus asks that this experience, his last meal with his followers, be commemorated, though it should be noted that the Passover was already a feast of remembrance (see Exodus 12.14). The *Catechism* states: 'By doing so, the Lord institutes his apostles as priests of the New Covenant: "For their sakes I sanctify myself, so that they also may be sanctified in truth".'[4] This comment is interpreted as referring to the apostles' priestly role in the commemoration. However, when St Paul talks about the commemoration of Jesus' sacrifice in a letter, it is addressed to the faithful: 'For as often as you eat this bread and drink the cup, you proclaim the Lord's death until he comes' (1 Corinthians 11.26). There is no mention of any person in a priestly role leading or presiding over the ritual, but rather a request to the Corinthians to participate in the commemoration in a respectful manner.

In three accounts, the Last Supper or Jewish Passover meal occurs before Jesus' death and resurrection (Matthew 26.26–29; Mark 14.22–25; Luke 22.1). In Mark's account,

Jesus follows the customary ritual carried out by the host of a Jewish meal by giving thanks. The Eucharist scenes are then described:

> While they were eating, he took a loaf of bread, and after blessing it he broke it, gave it to them, and said, 'Take; this is my body.' Then he took a cup, and after giving thanks he gave it to them, and all of them drank from it. He said to them, 'This is my blood of the covenant, which is poured out for many.' (Mark 14.22–24)

Matthew's account is almost identical:

> While they were eating, Jesus took a loaf of bread, and after blessing it he broke it, gave it to the disciples, and said, 'Take, eat; this is my body.' Then he took a cup, and after giving thanks he gave it to them, saying, 'Drink from it, all of you; for this is my blood of the covenant, which is poured out for many for the forgiveness of sins.' (Matthew 26.26–28)

In the Gospel of Luke, the request by Jesus to celebrate the meal in remembrance of him in the future is added:

> Then he took a loaf of bread, and when he had given thanks, he broke it and gave it to them, saying, 'This is my body, which is given for you. Do this in remembrance of me.' And he did the same with the cup after supper, saying, 'This cup that is poured out for you is the new covenant in my blood.' (Luke 22.19–20)

John's gospel offers a quite different version of events. Here, Jesus gives a long address on the subject of the bread from heaven to a crowd at a synagogue at Capernaum, in which he repeats: 'I am the bread of life' (John 6.35; 6.48). He then says: 'Those who eat my flesh and drink my blood have eternal life and I will raise them up on the last day; for my flesh is true food and my blood is true drink. Those who eat my flesh and drink my blood abide in me, and I in them' (John 6.54–56). While the words used by Jesus echo those recounted in the synoptic gospels, the discourse does not take place at a meal. In addition, the final meal that Jesus eats with the disciples in this gospel takes place before the Passover. In this account also, Jesus washes the disciples' feet (John 13.1–11) and goes on to deliver a long monologue about his betrayal and Peter's denial of him, a speech that is not replicated in the other gospel accounts.

In *The Ordination of Women in the Catholic Church*, John Wijngaards explains that at the Last Supper Jesus indicates a new age by using the words 'blood of the covenant' (Matthew 26.28; Mark 14.24; Luke 22.20). Blood was used symbolically to represent the seal of the covenant or the promise between God and Israel, with Israel symbolising the people of God. In other words, Jesus promises a new relationship between God and the people. In this context, the twelve apostles represent the twelve tribes of Israel and the twelve sons of Jacob. They are symbolic of the beginning of the new Israel or people of God. Their maleness, therefore, is not the point. It is the new era that is significant. Besides, a new tribe cannot be created without the participation of both sexes! In addition, according to Jewish law, women would have been present at the Passover meal: in this case, the Last Supper. It is more likely, in my view, that Jesus' request to 'do this in remembrance of me' was addressed, not only to the disciples, but to all his followers, present and future. We can be certain that Jesus asked that his sacrifice for us be commemorated, and that by doing so we would have the promise of eternal life. What we do not have are instructions about who should lead the commemoration ritual in the future. In my view, the request to remember and commemorate his sacrifice is the significant part. I find it difficult to see in these scenes the establishment of a perpetual male-only priesthood.

After the resurrection, eleven apostles or disciples, as Judas' successor had not yet been chosen, are sent out as missionaries by Jesus. The scenes described are similar in the various accounts. Mark recounts that after the resurrection Jesus appears to the eleven, 'and he upbraided them for their lack of faith and stubbornness, because they had not believed the women's testimony. And he said to them, "Go into all the world and proclaim the good news to the whole creation"' (Mark 16.14–15). Note here that the male apostles were not the first witnesses to the risen Jesus, a topic we shall return to later.

Similar instructions about spreading the good news are given in Matthew. After the resurrection, Jesus tells the eleven:

> All authority in heaven and on earth has been given to me. Go therefore and make disciples of all nations, baptizing them in the name of the Father and of the Son and of the Holy Spirit and teaching them to obey everything that

I have commanded you. And remember, I am with you always, to the end of the age. (Matthew 28.18–20)

The final sentence, Jesus' promise, is significant, as we shall discuss shortly. In Luke's gospel, the commissioning is not as explicit as in the other accounts. After the resurrection, Jesus speaks to 'the eleven and their companions'. There is a possibility that 'the companions' mentioned here include Mary Magdalene and some of the women who witnessed Jesus' suffering and death. Jesus recounts what was foretold about his death and resurrection. As a result of his suffering, he tells them, 'repentance and forgiveness of sins is to be proclaimed in his name to all nations, beginning from Jerusalem. You are witnesses of these things' (Luke 24.47– 48). In this account, it is the role of witness to the events that is emphasised.

Finally, in John's gospel, Jesus appears to the disciples three times after the resurrection, after first appearing and speaking to Mary Magdalene (John 20.11–18). When he then appears to the disciples, he says: "As the Father has sent me, so I send you." When he had said this, he breathed on them and said to them, "Receive the Holy Spirit. If you forgive the sins of any, they are forgiven them; if you retain the sins of any, they are retained"' (John 20.21–23). What is key here, to my mind, is that the receptor of the Holy Spirit is a conduit for the gift of healing and the forgiveness of sins. Additionally, most scholars agree that the words spoken by Jesus in this gospel are a reflection of the understanding of Jesus that had developed in the Christian communities, rather than an account of his actual words. What is significant, however, is that there is no specific 'ordination' ceremony or ritual carried out by Jesus that bears any resemblance to that enacted today. Jesus does not lay hands on the apostles or disciples. Notably, the word 'priest' is not used in the various accounts, even though there is a Greek word for priest as well as priestess. The words used most frequently are disciple and apostle.

However, current teaching specifies a priestly role, reserved for men and linked directly to the twelve. In his Apostolic Letter to the Bishops of the Catholic Church, *On Reserving Priestly Ordination to Men Alone: Ordinatio Sacerdotalis* (22 May 1994), John Paul II wrote:

> These men did not in fact receive only a function which could thereafter be exercised by any member of the Church; rather they were specifically and intimately associated in the mission of the Incarnate Word himself (cf. Mt 10:1, 7–8; 28:16–20; Mk 3:13–16; 16:14–15).[5]

In other words, only 'these men' are pertinent and all others, whether followers, prophets, prophetesses, witnesses, founders or leaders of communities, mentioned in the gospels and in St Paul's letters, are not 'intimately associated' in the mission to teach the word of God, because they were not specifically 'chosen' by twelve specific men, who in turn chose other men. It is not clear, therefore, how we are supposed to interpret the numerous other leadership roles mentioned in the scriptures.

AFTER JESUS: APOSTOLIC SUCCESSION

The next area of investigation is the successors of the twelve, as the *Catechism* is specific about the fact that the twelve apostles chose leaders to succeed them. Apostolic succession is defined as follows:

> In order that the full and living Gospel might always be preserved in the Church the apostles left bishops as their successors. They gave them 'their own position of teaching authority'. Indeed, 'the apostolic preaching, which is expressed in a special way in the inspired books, was to be preserved in a continuous line of succession until the end of time'.[6]

The quotations included in this definition are not taken from the scriptures, but rather from a document by Pope Paul VI (1963–78), entitled *Dogmatic Constitution On Divine Revelation: Dei Verbum* (18 November 1965). John Paul II, building on Paul VI's document (rather than drawing from the scriptures), went on to provide a fuller explanation of succession in *Ordinatio Sacerdotalis* (22 May 1994). After stating that the apostles were given a 'function' that applied only to them, John Paul II explained that this function is 'specifically and intimately associated in the mission of the Incarnate Word himself'.[7] Because the mission relates strictly to the chosen apostles, he continued, they passed it on specifically to their chosen successors: 'The Apostles did the same when they chose fellow workers (cf. 1 Timothy 3:1–13; 2 Timothy 1:6; Titus 1:5–9)[8] who would succeed them in their ministry.'[9] This was to be the pattern 'until the end of time'. However, no scene paralleling the *Catechism* description above occurs in the scriptures.

The 'living transmission' is understood to be the handing on of the gospel or good news from God/Jesus and the Holy Spirit to the apostles, and from the apostles to their successors. The successors are either those appointed by the apostles or, so that St Paul can be included here, those associated with them. The idea is that this teaching authority is, as explained in the *Catechism*, 'preserved in a continuous line of succession until the end of time'.[10] All of the above is prompted by the Holy Spirit, which, of course, in the institutional mind-set of the Church, prompts only men to serve God in ordained ministry. How this works is explained in the *Catechism*:

> This living transmission, accomplished in the Holy Spirit, is called Tradition, since it is distinct from Sacred Scripture, though closely connected to it. Through Tradition, 'the Church, in her doctrine, life and worship, perpetuates and transmits to every generation all that she herself is, all that she believes'.[11]

Tradition therefore serves as a bridge linking the scriptures and the interpretation of them. In other words, Tradition is separate from the gospel accounts but in some way still connected to them. You will note the use of 'all that she believes', which is, of course, where the problem lies, as it is the Church's belief that the exclusion of women is 'in accordance with God's plan for his Church'. As no prohibition is set down in the scriptures, the notion of Tradition is used here to authorise and support this teaching.

The next point to consider, therefore, is the apostles choosing their successors, in imitation of Jesus. Bear in mind that Luke recounts that Jesus sent out seventy others as missionaries, while John's account omits a detailed commissioning scene. Moreover, Jesus does not appear to specify that future disciples should be chosen deliberately by an overseer or bishop, or indeed by one of the apostles. In my view, the evidence to support the teaching that 'the apostles took care to appoint successors'[12] as the establishment of a tradition of a preserved apostolic preaching is tenuous, to say the least.

Acts of the Apostles recounts that when a replacement is chosen for Judas, two men are proposed. The successor is not chosen by the apostles, but rather, 'together with certain women, including Mary the mother of Jesus', and a crowd of about 120 believers (Acts 1.12–26). In other words, a collective decision is made to choose Judas' successor, Matthias. Also described in Acts is an account of seven men being selected to share the workload. The men are not chosen by the apostles but rather by 'the whole community of the disciples' (Acts 6.2). In contrast, the process of appointing bishops today is not by any stretch of the imagination a democratic one, such as that described in Acts.

Another piece of evidence employed by the Church is taken from Acts of the Apostles, where St Paul gives a farewell speech to the elders of the Church in Ephesus prior to his arrest in Jerusalem. Paul tells them: 'Keep watch over yourselves and over all the flock, of which the Holy Spirit has made you overseers, to shepherd the church of God that he obtained with the blood of his own Son' (Acts 20.28). It is not clear that Paul means 'overseer' as a specific office here. Moreover, overseers or elders do not appear to have been called to serve by Paul, or indeed by any other apostle for that matter.

Besides, Paul is not an apostle in the sense of having been chosen by Jesus or by one of Jesus' apostles, but rather is a disciple who felt he had been called to serve. He was not specifically 'commissioned' by one of the apostles. He was a convert who had formerly, as a Pharisee, persecuted Christians. Paul described his vocation at the beginning of his letter to the Romans:

> Paul, a servant of Jesus Christ, called to be an apostle, set apart for the gospel of God ... through whom we have received grace and apostleship to bring about the obedience of faith among all the Gentiles for the sake of his name (Romans 1.1–5).

In the first letter to Timothy, which is also cited in the argument for apostolic succession, the author, while extolling the traits of a good minister to his audience, writes: 'Do not neglect the gift that is in you, which was given to you through prophecy with the laying on of hands by the council of elders' (1 Timothy 4.14). This letter was, as mentioned earlier, attributed to Paul, but is now thought by many to have been composed early in the second century. The *HarperCollins Study Bible* explains that this pastoral letter, along with the second letter to Timothy and letter to Titus were written as a collection that were to be read together. As with Acts, it is extremely unlikely that all of the elders referred to in this letter were individually chosen successors of the apostles. Furthermore, in the second letter to Timothy, the author, who calls himself Paul, acknowledges the role of Timothy's mother and grandmother in giving Timothy the faith, and advises: 'For this reason I remind you to rekindle the gift of God that is within you through the laying on of my hands' (2 Timothy 1.5–6). However, as the identity of the author of the letter is unknown, there is no evidence to ascertain whether he himself had been appointed as a successor by one of the apostles. Similarly, in the third pastoral letter, letter to Titus, which is also concerned with instructions for behaviour and leadership in the community, it appears that the addressee, Titus, had been left to oversee the newly established community in Crete. But a mission to Crete by Paul is not mentioned in any of his letters or in Acts, thereby confirming the unlikelihood of either author or addressee being linked directly to Paul.

St Paul is deemed to be a teaching authority in the Church, yet he is not technically an apostle. He claimed his apostolic mission to be directly from the resurrected Jesus, and he was not sanctioned by one of the apostles. His words, in his letter to the Romans describing his initiation, indicate that he does not fit the criteria for the claiming of apostolic succession that is considered vital for the role of an authentic teacher in the Church. In Acts, the Lord Jesus appears to a disciple called Ananias, and tells him to go to Paul (still called Saul at this point), who has just seen a vision on the road to Damascus. There is no indication that Ananias, who is among a group of 'prophets and teachers' and is inspired by the Holy Spirit to lay hands on Paul, is a successor to one of the apostles. Ananias goes to Paul, lays hands on him and says: "'Brother Saul, the Lord Jesus, who appeared to you on your way here, has sent me so that you may regain your sight and be filled with the Holy Spirit." ... Then [Saul/Paul] got up and was baptized' (Acts 9.17–18). Later we are told about Saul/Paul's commissioning ceremony:

> Now in the church at Antioch there were prophets and teachers ... While they were worshiping the Lord and fasting, the Holy Spirit said, "Set apart for me Barnabas and Saul for the work to which I have called them." Then after fasting and praying they laid their hands on them and sent them off. (Acts 13.1–3)

This suggests that prophets, teachers and disciples could lay their hands on converts and 'ordain' them to do the Lord's work, which challenges the idea that only apostles and their specifically appointed successors can do so. As we shall see from Paul's letters, a variety of people – men, women and married couples – headed up the communities he founded. There is no evidence, therefore, that Paul understood these community leaders to be representatives of the continuance of a permanent male-only apostolic line of succession, exclusively invested with apostolic teaching.

Let us look at the Church's arguments in a little more detail. In Matthew's gospel, after the resurrection, in the scene where Jesus sends the disciples out as missionaries, he tells them: 'And remember, I am with you always to the end of the age' (Matthew 28.20). Jesus reassures the apostles and promises that he will always be with them. It should be noted that this is a promise that all the faithful receive through baptism. However, in this case, just as Jesus reassured Mary

Magdalene before leaving her, he does the same with the disciples. His promise, the *Catechism* explains, is the reference to the permanent aspect of the apostolic office:

> Christ promised to remain *with them* always. The divine mission entrusted by Jesus to them 'will continue to the end of time, since the Gospel they handed on is the lasting source of all life for the Church. Therefore … the apostles took care to appoint successors'.[13]

It is difficult to imagine why Jesus would mean this promise as him being with the eleven, and then specifically only with the successors that the eleven would directly appoint to succeed them. After all, how could the apostles ensure that particular chosen successors would 'hand on' the gospel? It is more likely that Jesus meant that he would be with the apostles *and* with whoever might spread the good news in the future, as well as the baptised faithful, as he also promises: 'For where two or three are gathered in my name, I am there among them' (Matthew 18.20).

The *Catechism* brings another strand to the argument for the idea of an unbroken apostolic succession: 'the Gospel they handed on is the lasting source of all life for the Church'.[14] There are some difficulties with this explanation of the apostles alone handing on the good news to specifically 'ordained' people. Jesus asked the apostles to spread the good news, and he also spoke about the costs and demands of following him as well as the nature of discipleship: 'If any want to become my followers, let them deny themselves and take up their cross daily and follow me' (Luke 9.23).[15] Furthermore, in Luke's gospel, Jesus speaks about the nature of discipleship. He does not specify those who may not qualify to follow him. He does not at any point explain that, for various reasons, some people are ineligible to be followers or missionaries. Rather, his words imply that the work of God is open to all who are called by the Holy Spirit.

If, as the Church argues, Jesus, inspired by the Holy Spirit, chose men to spread the good news and *only* men to carry out this undertaking in an official capacity, then it follows that the Church believes that the Holy Spirit does not call women to serve. However, there is a significant episode, as well as a speech attributed to Simon Peter, in Acts of the Apostles that casts doubt on this belief. It is the day of Pentecost and all the believers who are gathered together in Jerusalem are, we are told, filled with the Holy Spirit. Let us look a little more closely at these 'believers'. Acts lists the names of the apostles and adds: 'All these were constantly devoting themselves to prayer, together with certain women, including Mary the mother of Jesus, as well as his brothers' (Acts 1.14). Women, therefore, are present. On the day of Pentecost 'they were all together' when what looked like tongues of fire rested on each person there: 'All of them were filled with the Holy Spirit' (Acts 2.1–4). It is not specified here that the Holy Spirit made sure that the women present were not accidentally 'filled with the Holy Spirit' and thereby inspired to go out and teach!

In any case, after the believers have been 'filled with the Holy Spirit', a crowd gathers when they hear the believers begin to speak in tongues. Peter addresses the crowd: 'In the last days it will be, God declares, that I will pour out my Spirit upon all flesh, and your sons and your daughters shall prophesy ... Even upon my slaves, both men and women, in those days I will pour out my Spirit; and they shall prophesy' (Acts 2.17–18). Here, it is specified that status or gender, slave or free, male or female, are not barriers to the gift of prophesy. On another occasion, Peter declares: 'I truly understand that God shows no partiality, but in every nation anyone who fears him and does what is right is acceptable to him' (Acts 10.34–5). In other words, not only are Gentiles welcome, thereby specifying that God is not bigoted or racist, but there are no social or gender barriers either. Despite God showing 'no partiality', his followers do when it comes to women in priestly ministry or in any other leadership role.

The accounts above suggest the difficulty of ascertaining that the apostles, and indeed Paul, specifically chose male successors in the context of a deliberate permanent apostolic function. Indeed, the stories relating to spreading the good news suggest that oral accounts from many different witnesses, which were eventually written down, are the source for the various gospel accounts that preserve the teachings of Jesus. It seems highly unlikely, therefore, that 'apostolic preaching' was 'preserved in a continuous line of succession'. In short, our explorations so far suggest that the establishment of an elite band of male leaders called priests led by an even more elite band of men called bishops, based on examples from the gospels, is a long shot. Yet certain phrases have been interpreted by the Church to indicate that specific bishops were chosen and appointed by the apostles to act as overseers in their place.

In contrast, the examples we have looked at suggest that there was more than one way of being 'ordained' as a follower of Jesus. In *Can We Save the Catholic Church? We Can Save the Catholic Church!*, theologian Hans Küng summarises the evidence for the call to serve God as follows:

> Ministers are called by other ministers; the laying on of hands is carried out by prophets and teachers as well as by apostles (Acts); receiving a charismatic calling to exercise leadership in the community (1 Corinthians 12.28; 16.15); receiving a charismatic calling to preside over the community worship services (Romans 12.8).[16]

In other words, the specific appointing of a successor by an apostle is not the case.

Acts of the Apostles and the letters of St Paul (who was executed around AD 60–62) suggest that the call to work for Christ was the initial key component of missionary work. St Paul did not claim direct apostolic succession. Yet the Church teaches that bishops act as its shepherds and are direct representatives of the original apostles. The *Catechism* states: 'Hence the Church teaches that "the bishops have by divine institution taken the place of the apostles as pastors of the Church, in such wise that whoever listens to them is listening to Christ".'[17] As a result, the office of bishop is imbued with an authority claimed to be founded on the dual roles of Simon Peter as first witness and as Bishop of Rome. We shall now examine the evidence for this teaching.

SIMON PETER, FIRST WITNESS AND BISHOP OF ROME

Simon Peter is the chosen leader of the Roman Catholic Church as, it is taught, he was the first Bishop of Rome and the most important witness to the Christian story as well as to Jesus' words and deeds. Here is the description of the resurrection that is included in the *Catechism*:

> Mary Magdalene and the holy women who came to finish anointing the body of Jesus, which had been buried in haste because the Sabbath began on the evening of Good Friday, were the first to encounter the Risen One. Thus the women were the first messengers of Christ's Resurrection for the apostles themselves. They were the next to whom Jesus appears: first Peter, then the Twelve. Peter had been called to strengthen the faith of his brothers, and so sees the Risen One before them; it is on the basis of his testimony that the community exclaims: 'The Lord has risen indeed, and has appeared to Simon!'[18]

The last line in the passage above is taken from Luke's gospel, the only one that does not specify Mary Magdalene as first witness. Note here that the women's roles as messengers are now framed in gender-specific terms. They tell the apostles, the authority figures, about what they saw. In this way, their roles as first witnesses are implicitly downgraded to that of witness 'for the apostles'. Moreover, the women's testimony or message has to go through the apostles, specifically Peter; not because the disciples had deserted Jesus and so were not around, but rather for validation. In this way, the women become an instrument for the transmission of the news of the resurrection between Jesus and the apostles rather than being key witnesses of the event. It is a subtle repositioning of the status of first witness, and Simon Peter is now firmly positioned as the key person in the description of events.

St Paul's description of the event, in his letter to the Corinthians, also fails to specify Mary Magdalene as the first witness:

> For I handed on to you as of first importance what I in turn had received: that Christ died for our sins in accordance with the scriptures, and that he was buried, and that he was raised on the third day in accordance with the scriptures, and that he appeared to Cephas [Peter], then to the twelve. (1 Corinthians 15.3–5)

We now have two sources naming Simon Peter as the key person for the purpose of reinforcing his claim to leadership within the Church: Luke's gospel and St Paul's letter. It is these accounts that were consolidated into what is now the authoritative version, as given in the *Catechism*, despite the primacy of Mary Magdalene in the three other gospel accounts. Also, it is Peter's role as witness to the life and resurrection of Jesus that is deemed to be of central importance.

It should be noted that St Paul includes an account of the risen Jesus appearing to over 500 people, as well as the apostles and others, as mentioned earlier: 'All these were constantly devoting themselves to prayer, together with certain women, including Mary the mother of Jesus, as well as his brothers' (Acts 1.14). Despite the evidence of an array of witnesses, only the apostles who had known Jesus, it was argued, could claim the truth of his resurrection. As a result, other gospel accounts of visions of, or appearances by, Jesus, or the fact that many other people besides the twelve had also known the actual Jesus, were downplayed to give authority to the twelve, and in particular to Simon Peter.

The *Catechism* consolidates the exclusiveness of the apostles' role by stating: 'In the office of the apostles there is one aspect that cannot be transmitted: to be the chosen witnesses of the Lord's Resurrection and so the foundation stones of the Church.'[19] This rather random sleight of hand, with the inclusion of the word 'chosen', neatly dispenses with Mary Magdalene and the many others who saw the risen Jesus and were therefore witnesses to his resurrection. Additionally, it is a useful interpretation for suppressing any claim to authority by women. It was important to have this one aspect in the office of the apostles that 'cannot be transmitted'. This was because being witness to the resurrected Jesus became synonymous with authority.

The Gnostic texts present a different point of view in relation to witnesses of the resurrection, as well as the resurrection itself. As Elaine Pagels explains, rather than taking the resurrection literally, the idea was put forward that the event was about experiencing the presence of Jesus at any time rather than actually having seen him.[20] In other words, it was posited that some interpreters were mistaking a spiritual truth for an actual event. In that context, the texts explained, we do not have to physically die to be resurrected. Rather, a resurrection can be experienced at any time during a person's life, at a moment of enlightenment. As a result of these interpretations, and to shore up various claims to 'Truth', the Church moved to eliminate accounts other than those thought to have been composed by the apostles, in which people claimed to have seen Jesus in a vision or to have felt his presence. The concern was that, if anyone could experience a resurrection, then equally anybody could claim apostolic authority. In a hierarchical society, spurious claims to authority were unacceptable.

In the second century it was decided that only witnesses who had actually known Jesus could be deemed the official leaders of the Christian community. Consequently, Irenaeus, Bishop of Lyons, decreed that only those who could claim succession from the apostles, who had known Jesus, could be true bishops, as only they, he said, are vested with the 'gift of truth'.[21] One way around the problem of multiple witnesses in the claim for apostolic authority was therefore to claim authenticity for the four gospels thought to have been written by actual apostles, Matthew and John, or those deemed to be authentic followers of the apostles, Mark and Luke. John's gospel, for example, records an event where the risen Christ tells Peter to carry on his work (John 21.15–19), while Luke's account supports notions of authority bestowed on Simon Peter as a result of seeing the resurrected Jesus. These accounts therefore provided justification for hierarchical ideas that invested a small band of people with 'authoritarian' leadership, as well as vesting these leaders or apostles with the sole right to ordain future leaders or successors.

Of course, we now know that the four gospels cannot be proved to have been written by these particular men. However, Luke's account, proclaiming that the resurrected Jesus had appeared first to Simon (Luke 24.34) was used, as Pagels writes, 'to set the groundwork for establishing specific, restricted chains of command for all future generations of Christians. Any potential leader of the community would have to derive, or claim to derive, authority from the same apostles.'[22] This move to establish some sort of authority by the orthodox side of the Church, which began in the second century, restricted leadership to a very small band of people whose authority was, as a result of their status as witnesses, incontestable. As a result, the *Catechism* teaches that apostolic testimony is authentic and has more authority than any individual experience of God. Pagels summarises the theory as follows: '[A]ll authority derives from certain apostles' experience of the resurrected Christ, an experience now closed forever.'[23] As these 'certain apostles' were men, the Church has assumed that the experience is 'closed forever' to women.

It is a point of faith that popes are successors of Simon Peter as Bishop of Rome. As the *Catholic Dictionary* explains, 'the divinely appointed primacy of St. Peter has been entrusted to each successor who has taken his place. The pope, as the Bishop of Rome, is considered "another Peter" and, therefore, the head of the College of Bishops.'[24] Thus we are taught that the papacy is founded on the office of Peter as Bishop of Rome. The Roman claim to primacy was based on the interpretation of the words of Jesus contained in one synoptic gospel account: 'And I tell you, you are Peter, and on this rock I will build my church, and the gates of Hades will not prevail against it' (Matthew 16.18). This line in Matthew's gospel is one of only two passages in the gospels where the word 'church' is used (see also Matthew 18.17). As Jesus usually talks about the kingdom of God, it can be argued that the word 'church', with only two occurrences in the New Testament, was probably added at a later date.

The context of this passage, wherein Jesus is purported to have vested supreme authority in Peter, is part of a discussion that takes place between Jesus and the disciples. Jesus asks the disciples what is being said about him, and on hearing Peter's reply, Jesus praises him for his faith in declaring him the Messiah. Jesus' words, quoted above, reward that faith. As the Greek word for rock and Peter are one and the same, it seems likely that Jesus is conferring gifts on Peter himself and on the work he will do for the Lord and the kingdom of God, rather than on attaching significance to any particular place where he might teach in the future, or indeed on Peter as an authority figure. Tellingly, when the disciples argue on the way to Capernaum about which of them is the greatest (Mark 9.35), Jesus is quick to admonish them. He is quite clear in his views about assuming authority over others and this is underlined by the repetition of this teaching in the same gospel:

> So Jesus called them and said to them, 'You know that among the Gentiles those whom they recognize as their rulers lord it over them, and their great ones are tyrants over them. But it is not so among you; but whoever wishes to become great among you must be your servant, and whoever wishes to be first among you must be slave of all.' (Mark 10.42–44)

There is little evidence in these words to support the authoritarian leadership invested in Peter by the later Church.

Moreover, it is not certain that St Peter was ever Bishop of Rome. St Paul, in his letter to the Romans, written around AD 58, does not include Peter in his greeting, making it unlikely that Peter was residing there at the time. Peter is thought to have been executed in Rome between AD 64 and 67, thus rendering a long period of time living in Rome impossible. Eusebius of Caesarea (AD 260/265–339/340), who is credited as the earliest writer of Church history, never refers to Peter as Bishop of Rome. Additionally, Irenaeus, Bishop of Lyons, who enumerated all the Roman bishops up to the twelfth, Eleutherius, does not include him. According to Irenaeus, as Peter de Rosa writes in *Vicars of Christ*, 'the first bishop of Rome was not Peter or Paul but Linus. The Apostolic Constitution in the year 270 also named Linus as first bishop of Rome, appointed by St Paul. After Linus came Clement, chosen by Peter.'[25] Thus Paul appointed Linus as Bishop of Rome, and Peter then appointed Clement. This suggests that Paul and Peter did not see the role of Bishop of Rome as a claim for some sort of primacy over all other Christian communities.

The role of bishop does not appear to have been particularly significant in the early Church. Mark Humphries writes: '[I]t was only in the late second century, or even the early third, that a bishop with authority over all Rome's Christians finally emerged.'[26] As discussed earlier, the First Ecumenical Council at Nicaea in 325 was convened by Emperor Constantine without any reference to the bishops. In other words, the emperor was the authority, not the Bishop of Rome or any other bishop. It appears, therefore, that notions of hierarchical authority were not invested in Peter or in Rome at the time in the way they are today. Rather, Peter was one part of the entire missionary Church, with no particular significance being attached to him or to where he might be teaching.

The claim for the special status of Rome over any other city is based on fourth-century Church documents and followed on from the 'special authority' bestowed on the Church leaders of Alexandria, Antioch and Rome at the Council of Nicaea. The Apostolic Constitutions, which are concerned with the governance and discipline of the early church, were the most extensive canonical and liturgical compilations ever composed. The documents stemmed, it was mooted, from the apostles, which is now known to be impossible. However, they were hugely influential, because of their supposed authorship, and were later incorporated into an ecclesiastical code, *Concordia discordantium canonum* (Concordance of Discordant Canons), compiled by the twelfth-century monk and lawyer Gratian of Bologna, who is reputed to be the father of Canon Law. The claim for special status mirrored the merging of ecclesiastical and imperial administration in cities, Humphries writes, 'that were also the headquarters of Roman administration in the provinces'.[27] Given the status of Rome over all other cities in the Empire, coupled with the seal of apostolic approval in the Apostolic Constitutions, the claim for the ecclesiastical authority of Rome was almost inevitable.

In light of these developments, at the beginning of the fifth century Bishop Innocent I of Rome (401–17) decided that all Church matters should be sent to him for approval and proclamation; if, of course, appropriate to his point of view. This notion of Rome's authority was not shared by churches in other jurisdictions, but Innocent and his successors continued to claim primacy and special status. Two popes who greatly increased the power of the papacy, and who ensured that power was centralised in Rome, were Gregory VII (1073–85) and Innocent III (1198–1216). Indeed, Gregory VII laid down twenty-seven principles to establish both his superiority and that of future pontiffs, while Innocent III, a contemporary of St Francis of Assisi, was responsible for adding 'Ruler of the World' to the list of pontifical titles. Thus our explorations show that the positioning of Rome as the supreme city leader and the primacy invested in Peter as Bishop of Rome is based on a tenuous claim. In short, as Hans Küng states: 'St Peter was not given a primacy of jurisdiction by Christ, nor did he exercise one in the Apostolic Church. Neither did he pass his special role in the Apostolic Church on to a direct historical successor.'[28]

Yet the supreme authority of the pope as successor to Peter is a central tenet of the Catholic Church: 'For the Roman Pontiff, by reason of his office as Vicar of Christ, and as pastor of the entire Church has full, supreme and universal power over the whole Church, a power which he can always exercise unhindered.'[29] The latter phrase in particular contradicts the collegial model of the early Christian movement that evolved from a willingness to spread the good news – by men and women, married and unmarried, sharing, discussing and interpreting, collectively, the work to be done.

We shall now turn our attention to the written arguments made by successive popes in their bid to close down the topic of the admission of female teachers and preachers to the Roman Catholic Church.

3

ALL ABOUT THE MAN

WE CANNOT ORDAIN WOMEN: AN OVERVIEW OF THE TOPIC

This chapter begins with a chronological summary of how the debate about women's ordination has played out. I should point out that much of what follows is not new information, as it has been widely researched and published by scholars, though much of it was new to me when beginning my research, despite being brought up as a Catholic. Thus I drew on the work of many eminent theologians and historians to explore the questions I had.

The question of the ordination of women to the priesthood has surfaced regularly since the 1960s, and attempts to quash it have been vigorous. The fact that the subject cannot be dismissed utterly is because the arguments given against it have not, in my view, proved to be either satisfactory or conclusive. I shall begin with a brief overview of how the topic has been addressed by the Vatican, from the 1960s up to the re-entrenchment of the Church's position on the ordination of women in 2010.

The 1960s was a time of social and cultural change. Personal autonomy was an achievable aim and women became visible in the public arena. While, on the one hand, the Church may be focused on 'tradition', it has, on the other, always been politically astute. In *Dei Verbum*, Pope Paul VI indirectly addressed the growing call from women about participating more visibly in the Church by reiterating the significance of the male gender throughout the document. The context is an explanation of revelation, which is how the Church interprets the way in which God makes himself and his purposes known to humanity. In other words, this authoritative teaching document addresses 'God's plan for his Church'. The deliberate exclusion of women from the priesthood, as inferred by the choosing of the twelve, is considered to be part of that plan. This idea was consequently incorporated by John Paul II into his explanation of the reasons for denying ordination to women: 'her living teaching authority which has consistently held that the exclusion of women from the priesthood is in accordance with God's plan for his Church'.[1]

In *Dei Verbum*, Pope Paul VI addressed the purpose of revelation:

> Through this revelation, therefore, the invisible God (see Col[ossians] 1:15; 1 Tim 1:17) out of the abundance of His love speaks to men as friends (see Ex 33:11; John 15:14–15) and lives among them (see Bar[uch] 3:38), so that He may invite and take them into fellowship with Himself.[2]

Paul VI explained that Jesus was sent to engage with men: 'Jesus Christ, therefore, the Word made flesh, was sent as "a man to men".'[3] Jesus' maleness becomes a central facet of the argument. While it was the convention to include women among the general terms 'mankind' or 'humankind', in this document the word 'men' is used throughout; over forty times in fact. The words 'woman' or 'women' are never used. In other words, by focusing on men and maleness, the exclusion of women is implicit. To read this passage as a woman, therefore, whatever the intended meaning, is to feel that God interacts only with men, and moreover only takes men 'into fellowship with Himself'.

There is more. The Pope continued:

> In composing the sacred books, God chose men and while employed by Him they made use of their powers and abilities, so that with Him acting in them and through them, they, as true authors, consigned to writing everything and only those things which He wanted.[4]

In short, only the unidentified men who wrote the gospels – the gospels chosen as the definitive texts by the institution from the second century onwards, that is – were given the special grace to speak and write on God's behalf, and most especially to write 'only those things which He wanted'. The Pope went on to explain how he and the teaching authority of the Church knew this:

> However, since God speaks in Sacred Scripture through men in human fashion, the interpreter of Sacred Scripture, in order to see clearly what God wanted to communicate to us, should carefully investigate what meaning the sacred writers really intended, and what God wanted to manifest by means of their words.[5]

In other words, the 'interpreter of Sacred Scripture' has to make an educated guess as to 'what God wanted' to say and teach. Moreover, the interpreter has to decide what the original writers 'really intended', presumably when the meaning is not clear, or is ambiguous. It is, therefore, all about interpretation, and the Church has decided that these men, by not writing about Jesus choosing a woman among the twelve, have shown that God's intent is that women may never be 'chosen'. Unfortunately, the authors of the particular scriptural texts did not elaborate on the role of Jesus' women followers. As men writing for men, they were focused on the doings of men alone.

Further written explanation in this regard was prompted by the Anglican Church's move to consider ordaining women, as this would have an impact on the ecumenical relationship between the two Churches. A letter, published in the official Gazette of the Holy See, *Acta Apostolicae Sedis* (*AAS*), written by Pope Paul VI to the Archbishop of Canterbury, the Most Reverend Dr F. D. Coggan (1974–80), expresses the Pope's concern. The Catholic Church, Pope Paul VI wrote:

> holds that it is not admissible to ordain women to the priesthood, for very fundamental reasons. These reasons include: the example recorded in the Sacred Scriptures of Christ choosing his Apostles only from among men; the constant practice of the Church, which has imitated Christ in choosing only men; and her living teaching authority which has consistently held that the exclusion of women from the priesthood is in accordance with God's plan for his Church.[6]

However, these reasons, as outlined in the previous chapter, no longer seemed clear-cut and, in a changing cultural landscape, were questioned rather than accepted.

In April 1976, because there were sustained rumblings about the matter, there was an interesting and significant development. The question had been posed again as to whether women could be ordained to priestly ministry, as ministers of the Eucharist or as leaders in the Christian community. As a result, the Vatican's Pontifical Biblical Commission was charged to study the evidence from the scriptures in light of this question. The commission, all of whom were ordained men (women or lay biblical scholars were not included), duly reported in 'Can Women Be Priests?' that its forensic examination of the scriptures could not answer the question one way or the other. In other words, no scriptural barrier could be found to women's ordination.[7]

In lieu of the Pontifical Biblical Commission's result, Paul VI ordered the Congregation for the Doctrine of the Faith (CDF), an all-male group made up of cardinals, archbishops and bishops, to look into the matter. The ensuing document, *Declaration on the Question of Admission of Women to the Ministerial Priesthood: Inter Insigniores* (15 October 1976), stated in its introduction that the Church 'does not consider herself authorized to admit women to priestly ordination'.[8] In other words, Jesus, God or the Holy Spirit has not given the Church explicit permission to ordain women. This is an extraordinary stance to take given the dearth of orders given by Jesus about anything. The document also reaffirmed the three arguments against women's ordination conveyed in Pope Paul VI's letter to the Archbishop of Canterbury.[9]

The subject of ecumenism was at the heart of the next exchange of views on the matter. In 1984 a series of four letters between Pope John Paul II and the Archbishop of Canterbury, Robert Runcie (1980–91), on the topic of the ordination of women, echoes the views expressed by Paul VI in the 1970s. The letters were published in *Origins*, the documentary service of the Catholic News Service, on 17 July 1986. John Paul II and Archbishop Runcie had prayed together in Canterbury Cathedral during the Pope's visit to Britain in 1982, and Runcie was strongly in favour of a good relationship between Rome and the Anglican Church. Much of Archbishop Runcie's archiepiscopate was taken up with the debate over whether to proceed with the ordination of women in the Church of England. The process was torturous.[10]

The main points of the correspondence between John Paul II and Archbishop Runcie are summarised by Mary T. Malone in *Women and Christianity*. Anglican discussions revolved around the following issues:

> The supposed masculinity of God and the maleness of Jesus were central to the discussions, as were the anthropological questions about the nature of women and their sexuality. The long-lasting Christian traditions about the damaged nature of women and their links with evil were invoked endlessly. The standard arguments about male headship over women, the status of women as daughters of Eve, the decrees in Corinthians and Timothy about the silence of women in the churches, and the supposedly continuous tradition against the ordination of women were endlessly

invoked, proved inconclusive or downright wrong and re-invoked by opponents with new arguments.[11]

All of the above are familiar themes and topics based on prejudices and traditional practice rather than on evolving interpretations. Malone relates that the Pope expressed the view that the Anglican Church's move to ordain women would hamper the great strides made in the relationship between the Churches. However, the eventual reply from Archbishop Runcie expressed the view that there were, 'in scripture and tradition no fundamental objections to the ordination of women'.[12] His view paralleled the similar finding of the Catholic Church's own Biblical Commission, noted earlier.

The Archbishop had other interesting points to make. He said that salvation for humanity, 'must be a humanity inclusive of women, if half the human race is to share in the redemption he won for us on the cross'.[13] Archbishop Runcie also addressed the idea in Catholic doctrine of the male-only priest as being representative of Christ. The Anglican view is that the minister is commissioned by the Church in ordination to represent Christ, and that the full humanity of Christ reflects a humanity consisting of male and female. Runcie went one step further, writing that 'most human societies have surrendered an exclusively male leadership, and as a result, "the representative nature of the ministerial priesthood is actually weakened by a solely male priesthood"'.[14] In other words, both Church and society need the attributes of male and female to flourish. Thus legislation was drafted in 1984 for women to be appointed to teaching and leadership roles in the Anglican Church. The response from Rome was to simply repeat the main doctrinal points from *Inter Insigniores*. The theological sticking point at the end of this exchange is that the Catholic Church argues that the ordained priest does not represent the priesthood of all the people, but rather stands in, as such, for Christ. As Christ is a man, only a man can represent him.

The appointment of women to ministry in the Anglican Church, and the growing strength of feminist voices, meant that the topic could not be dismissed as easily as before. Thus John Paul II addressed the matter once again in *On the Dignity and Vocation of Women on the Occasion of the Marian Year: Mulieris Dignitatem* (15 August 1988). The Pope wrote:

> In calling only men as his Apostles, Christ acted in a completely free and sovereign manner. In doing so, he exercised the same freedom with which, in all his behavior, he emphasized the dignity and the vocation of women, without conforming to the prevailing customs and to the traditions sanctioned by the legislation of the time.[15]

The Pope is arguing that while the 'prevailing customs' of the time were that women were inferior and servile, Jesus still spoke to, healed, interacted with and defended the women he met during his ministry. So, John Paul II goes on to stress, Jesus was implying that customs were irrelevant and by choosing men to be his representatives, therefore, he chose deliberately. By taking this position the Catholic Church, in contrast to the Anglican position, can argue that cultural contexts or advances are irrelevant in relation to this particular topic.

Personally, I am not sure how 'the dignity and the vocation of women' can be gleaned from a sentence that is based on notions of exclusion. In addition, the word 'vocation' is troubling, as it brings to mind the selfless, martyr-mother figure of old who lives for others and denies her own needs and desires. This in turn suggests that the status of women depends on being attached to others as wives and/or mothers rather than as human beings in their own right.

In *Ordinatio Sacerdotalis* (22 May 1994), John Paul II responded once again to the argument that it was the cultural conditions of the time rather than it being an edict to be followed for all time that Jesus deliberately chose men to follow him. This is, of course, if one disregards the presence and role of Mary Magdalene in the gospels. The Pope drew on the work of Pope Paul VI, who had directed the Congregation for the Doctrine of the Faith to set out and expound on the teaching of the Church on this matter in *Inter Insigniores*. John Paul II argued that *Inter Insigniores* showed clearly, 'that Christ's way of acting did not proceed from sociological or cultural motives peculiar to his time'.[16] Furthermore, the document, he said, had explained the matter as follows: 'The real reason is that, in giving the Church her fundamental constitution, her theological anthropology – thereafter always followed by the Church's Tradition – Christ established things in this way.'[17] You will note here how weighty authoritarian words such as 'fundamental' and 'theological' are employed to add importance to the arguments that have been put forward previously. In other words, the argument is that Jesus did not make his choice in the context of the times, in that choosing women would have been unthinkable, but rather, he was setting an example for all time by deliberately choosing men.

As will be appreciated, it takes quite a lot of explaining when you are arguing for the exclusion of half of the human race, so John Paul II had more to say about Jesus deliberately choosing male apostles for his mission:

> In fact the Gospels and the Acts of the Apostles attest that this call was made in accordance with God's eternal plan; Christ chose those whom he willed (cf. Mk 3:13–14; Jn 6:70), and he did so in union with the Father, 'through the Holy Spirit' (Acts 1:2), after having spent the night in prayer (cf. Lk 6:12). Therefore, in granting admission to the ministerial priesthood, the Church has always acknowledged as a perennial norm her Lord's way of acting in choosing the twelve men whom he made the foundation of his Church (cf. Rv 21:14).[18]

The point here is that the Church is arguing that it is taking Jesus' example of deliberately choosing men as the model for all time because Jesus was guided to do so by the Holy Spirit. The 'granting admission to the ministerial priesthood' quotation is not taken from the scriptures. Rather, it is from the *Dogmatic Constitution on the Church: Lumen Gentium* (Light of the Nations) (21 November 1964), one of the principal documents of the Second Vatican Council, promulgated by Pope Paul VI. The document expounds on the Church's nature, mission and structures as revealed in the scriptures, apostolic writings and various Vatican documents, and is an interpretation of the events in the scriptures in relation to ideas about the 'ministerial priesthood'.

Finally, on the topic of women in apostolic roles, John

Paul II argued that if there was to be a female apostle, only Our Lady would be suitable. Furthermore, women should not see their exclusion from ministry as a reflection of their lack of value in the Church:

> Furthermore, the fact that the Blessed Virgin Mary, Mother of God and Mother of the Church, received neither the mission proper to the Apostles nor the ministerial priesthood clearly shows that the non-admission of women to priestly ordination cannot mean that women are of lesser dignity, nor can it be construed as discrimination against them. Rather, it is to be seen as the faithful observance of a plan to be ascribed to the wisdom of the Lord of the universe. The presence and the role of women in the life and mission of the Church, although not linked to the ministerial priesthood, remain absolutely necessary and irreplaceable. As the *Declaration Inter Insigniores* points out, 'the Church desires that Christian women should become fully aware of the greatness of their mission: today their role is of capital importance both for the renewal and humanization of society and for the rediscovery by believers of the true face of the Church'.[19]

I am not sure how the 'greatness of their mission' can be achieved if women do not have any access to leadership roles in the Church. This patronising statement also affirms the importance of women's role in the 'humanization of society', while at the same time claiming that such a role is not needed in the Church organisation itself. This in turn suggests that the hierarchy believe they are doing a perfectly good job without the help of women.

What the Pope really means here is that women have one role, and in that role, as mothers, women are obliged to pass on the faith to their children. That is the reason why Mary, the mother of Jesus, is brought into the above statement. Mary was chosen to be the human mother of Jesus. That has nothing to do with apostolic mission. She has, therefore, in my view, no place in this particular discussion. However, it is reassuring to know that women are 'necessary and irreplaceable' in the life of the Church – just not in an administrative role, obviously, but perfectly acceptable when they have a tin of polish in their hands! Additionally, women's role to revitalise society and the Church is 'of capital importance', which basically reiterates their duty of being 'motherly' to all. The statement also appears to give women some type of responsibility for the perpetuation of the faith without actually giving them a ministerial role. John Wijngaards sums up the Church's contradictory stance succinctly: '[W]omen share fully in the apostolic mission of the Church, but Christ did not want them to be ministerial priests.'[20]

John Paul II concluded his thoughts on the matter with a crisp and authoritative order:

> Wherefore, in order that all doubt may be removed regarding a matter of great importance, a matter which pertains to the Church's divine constitution itself, in virtue of my ministry of confirming the brethren (cf. Lk 22:32) I declare that the Church has no authority whatsoever to confer priestly ordination on women and that this judgment is to be definitively held by all the Church's faithful.[21]

In other words, there is to be no more doubt about this matter. The Church cannot ordain women because Jesus did not show us that it can, and as the infallible leader of the Church, the pope's word is final.

John Paul II's command was repeated in a response issued by the then Cardinal Joseph Ratzinger, Prefect of the Congregation for the Doctrine of the Faith at that time. The Apostolic Letter, *Responsum ad Propositum Dubium Concerning the Teaching contained in "Ordinatio Sacerdotalis"* (28 October 1995) opened as follows:

> [T]he Church has no authority whatsoever to confer priestly ordination on women ... This teaching requires definitive assent, since, founded on the written Word of God, and from the beginning constantly preserved and applied in the Tradition of the Church, it has been set forth infallibly by the ordinary and universal Magisterium ... Thus, in the present circumstances, the Roman Pontiff, exercising his proper office of confirming the brethren (cf. Lk 22:32), has handed on this same teaching by a formal declaration, explicitly stating what is to be held always, everywhere, and by all, as belonging to the deposit of the faith.[22]

The doctrine of papal infallibility is invoked here with vigour. In short, the teaching is infallible and cannot be questioned. Furthermore, if you are a Catholic you must hold the view that the Church cannot ever ordain women to the priesthood.

Three years later, John Paul II took a new line of attack (or defence, depending on one's point of view) by issuing an Apostolic Letter, *Ad Tuendam Fidem* (To Defend the

Faith) (18 May 1998). The document authorised key additions to the Code of Canon Law and a number of changes were implemented. Changes to Canon Law are quite rare; in past centuries there have been only a few such alterations. In any case, John Paul II said that the changes were needed to 'protect the faith of the Catholic Church against errors arising from certain members of the Christian faithful'. One significant change was the demand that candidates for the office of bishop, theologian or papal collaborator recite an oath of loyalty, expressing belief in 'divinely revealed truths', as well as a belief in all teachings on faith and morals that have been 'definitively proposed by the Church'. One of the 'definite truths' is the ban on female priests. Candidates must also promise to 'adhere with religious submission of will and intellect' to future teachings announced by the pope and College of Bishops.[23] Existing prelates, parish priests, theology teachers and religious superiors are also required to take the oath. This is apparently in response to the many Roman Catholic theologians who have questioned or tried to re-examine Church teachings on topics such as female ordination, celibacy, artificial methods of birth control, premarital sex, homosexuality and so on. Transgressors are now subject to punishments ranging from warnings to excommunication. This is a huge step away from the collaborative nature of the early Church, another recurring issue given the objectives of collegiality set out at the Second Vatican Council.

Indeed, the notion of collaboration prompted the next development in the series of orders about the topic of female ordination. In 2004 the Congregation for the Doctrine of the Faith issued a letter to all bishops entitled 'Letter to the bishops of the Catholic Church on the Collaboration of Men and Women in the Church and in the World' (31 May 2004). Readers may be surprised to discover that the letter promotes women's roles in society and talks about the positive contribution that women make to the world in the public domain, a finding that has been borne out in various studies. However, any positives in the letter are soon undermined, as it goes on to reiterate that women's primary responsibilities are in the home as mothers – a role, they say, that should be recognised and valued by society. While this seems laudable, it can be said that it seems to be a case of putting the cart before the horse. Surely, women should be 'valued' in their own right before 'value' is applied to any role they might undertake? The letter then adopts a paternal tone by reassuring women that not only are they capable, but it is indeed their duty to pass on the good news to their children. But, of course, women cannot carry out this role on any formal footing within the Church.

The letter, as discussed and analysed by Professor Tina Beattie in the opening chapter of *New Catholic Feminism: Theology and Theory*, basically reasserts that old chestnut of 'natural law', whereby motherhood is deemed to be the ultimate aim for *all* women, and all men are naturally superior in terms of intellect and ability. I should explain 'natural law' at this point, as it is a theory that underpins the perception of women's status in the Catholic Church. Thomas Aquinas (c. 1225–74) incorporated natural law theory, a theory taken from the Ancient Greek philosopher Aristotle (384–322 BC) into Church thinking. Natural law is understood as a body of unchanging moral principles regarded as the basis for all human conduct. The *Catholic Dictionary* explains that 'Natural law is promulgated by God and is the "objective order" established by Him.' Order is understood here in terms of hierarchy. Part of that order is that there is a division between the private and public spheres, home and the outside world, with women being associated with home and domestic affairs, and men with public affairs. By incorporating ancient Greek philosophical ideology, Church Fathers, such as Thomas Aquinas, viewed the containment of women to the private realm as being complementary to the removal of the source of sin and temptation for men engaged in public affairs. As a result, Aquinas systematically defined natural law with the obligations and rights that constitute it, seeing the father as the head and ruler of his household, for example, and consequently responsible for its upkeep and the welfare of its members. This theory, therefore, understood world order as a well-regulated, patriarchal and hierarchical world order, and women had little place in this model.

To continue with the letter above, then, while on the one hand, women have an 'irreplaceable role … in all aspects of family and social life involving human relationships and caring for others',[24] on the other hand, this cannot apply to the Church. The Church, therefore, it can be argued, is unwittingly acknowledging that an 'irreplaceable' element is missing from its male-only hierarchy. If our role in human relationships is 'irreplaceable', why does it not apply to working with the people of God, who are the Church? The letter, therefore, is not really about collaboration at all, as it focuses largely on outdated ideas about the nature of women, which assumes their subjection to the male as taught by Thomas

Aquinas. Thus any comments about women's positive contribution to society are completely undermined. In addition, the letter addresses the topic of violence against women, but does not acknowledge the role of sexism in facilitating such violence.

Finally, in a breathtakingly contradictory summation of the supposed point of the letter, which is the call for collaboration, the Congregation for the Doctrine of the Faith state: 'The witness of women's lives must be received with respect and appreciation, as revealing those values without which humanity would be closed in self-sufficiency, dreams of power and the drama of violence.'[25] In other words, women must be valued for the positive attributes they bring to society, but there is no need for these attributes in the Church, as it, unlike society, apparently does not fall into the trap of 'self-sufficiency', 'power' or 'violence'. The letter reveals the mindset of an all-male group (Congregation for the Doctrine of the Faith) writing exclusively to another all-male group, the bishops, and confidently proclaiming themselves as 'expert in humanity' in the opening sentence of the letter.

These male 'expert[s] in humanity' judge that while women are valuable and 'irreplaceable', they are 'different'. This is the type of language formerly used in relation to racial difference. The word 'different' usually has negative qualities attached to it. Yet there is no outcry at this type of language when it concerns women. For example, John Paul II wrote in *Mulieris Dignitatem*: 'The personal resources of femininity are certainly no less than the resources of masculinity: they are merely different.'[26] No matter how much the value of women is lauded, the bottom line is that they are not seen by the institutional Church as having been created in the image of God in quite the same way as men. Basically, the encyclical repeats the essentialist gender argument about women – all women are the same – that has long been dispensed with in fields such as biology, anthropology, psychology and sociology.

In 2010 Benedict XVI attempted to close down the subject in a document, originally composed by Pope John Paul II in 2001, that contains a series of regulations or 'norms' and lists the most serious 'crimes' identified by the Church. In this edition, the ordination of women is included among the list of the most serious crimes in Church law. *A brief introduction to the modifications made in the Normae de gravioribus delictis* (21 May 2010) states: 'The attempted ordination of a woman has also been introduced as a delict in the new text, as established by the decree of the Sacred Congregation for the Doctrine of the Faith on 19 December 2007 (art. 5)'.[27] A delict is a crime or violation of Canon Law. The overhaul of the Penal Code of Canon Law, wherein the penalties for the breaking of Canon Laws are listed, also reaffirmed the sanction of excommunication for anyone involved with the ordination of women in the Catholic Church. The Congregation for the Doctrine of the Faith had stated in May 2008 that women priests and the bishops who ordained them would be excommunicated *latae sententiae*, that is, automatically. The new decree goes one step further and enshrines the action as 'a crime against sacraments', which is in the same category as clerical child abuse. This was to be the final word on the matter and the message was transmitted to the faithful with all the authority available to the institutional Church.

Readers might be interested to know that while the Church was reiterating its decisive opposition to women's ordination, it was, from 1992 onwards, conducting discussions with disenchanted Anglican clergymen unhappy with the admission of women to ordination in their Church. The question of how to admit married clergy to the Catholic priesthood was a key topic in light of the Catholic Church's celibacy rule. However, it was eventually overcome, and thus, in the same year (2010) as the 'crime' of ordaining Catholic women to the priesthood was elevated, Pope Benedict XVI offered an invitation to disillusioned Anglicans to convert to Catholicism while still keeping tenets of their own faith. The *Personal Ordinariate of Our Lady of Walsingham*, established by Pope Benedict XVI in 2011, facilitates the ordination of Anglican clergymen to the Catholic priesthood, so that being married is no obstacle to their ordination and subsequent ministry in the Catholic Church.

This invitation to Anglicans was accepted by some of their clergy. Fiona Govan, writing about the victory of the vote against proceeding with women bishops in the Anglican Church in England, reported: 'About 60 traditionalist clergy, including five male bishops, and about 900 lay members have already switched to the Roman Catholic Church after Pope Benedict welcomed those who had become alienated by the prospect of the changes.'[28] Clearly, the people who have 'switched' to Catholicism are confident that the Roman Catholic Church will not embrace inclusiveness, as did their former Church, but will continue to focus on notions of exclusivity. Considering the traditional antipathy towards Rome by the British in particular, the conversion to Roman Catholicism by former Anglicans illustrates the extent of the misogyny still present in the Christian world-view. In other words, these new recruits find the idea of having female colleagues in ministry so distasteful that they are willing to convert from one religion to another.

From a female perspective, what does this open-armed invitation to former Anglicans tell Catholic women about how they are viewed by the Catholic Church hierarchy? It tells them that a disenchanted married man from another tradition is more acceptable than a woman from the Catholic Church's own fold. It seems that not only are Catholic women inferior to Catholic men, they are also inferior to men of other faiths in the eyes of the Church into which they have been baptised. Are women, in fact, considered real or proper Catholics at all?

The appointment of Pope Francis I in 2013 does not herald any change with regard to the male priesthood. In his apostolic exhortation entitled *Evangelii Gaudium* (The Joy of the Gospel) (24 November 2013) Pope Francis, as is wearyingly customary, begins his remarks by listing female attributes, which usually precede the clichés, as these attributes revert to the essentialist view of women's nature. However, he does accept that women must have a role in public life. An apostolic exhortation, by the way, is one of the most authoritative categories of papal documents. Pope Francis writes:

> The Church acknowledges the indispensable contribution which women make to society through the sensitivity, intuition and other distinctive skill sets which they, more

than men, tend to possess. I think, for example, of the special concern which women show to others, which finds a particular, even if not exclusive, expression in motherhood. I readily acknowledge that many women share pastoral responsibilities with priests, helping to guide people, families and groups and offering new contributions to theological reflection. But we need to create still broader opportunities for a more incisive female presence in the Church. Because 'the feminine genius is needed in all expressions in the life of society, the presence of women must also be guaranteed in the workplace' and in the various other settings where important decisions are made, both in the Church and in social structures.[29]

As usual, 'womanly' attributes that are expressed particularly 'in motherhood' are lauded. And women's 'presence' in the world, outside the home, is also finally acknowledged by the Vatican. The Pope even hints that women's 'presence' might be a beneficial one in 'settings where important decisions are made'. There might even be room for the 'feminine genius' in the Church. That remark, of course, should placate women for another few hundred years while the question of opening the diaconate to women is considered! It may surprise readers to know that Pope John Paul II also recognised that there was cultural inequality with regard to women, and, moreover, that Jesus' example and the scriptures supported the involvement of women in ecclesial life.[30]

However, the fear that including women to any extent would lead to a call for wider participation, or indeed admission to the priesthood, is probably the sticking point to practising what the Church preaches about the value of women. This, it can be argued, is why the praising of women's virtues is always tempered with cautionary remarks. For example, in the same exhortation in which Pope Francis lists women's virtues, he continues:

> Demands that the legitimate rights of women be respected, based on the firm conviction that men and women are equal in dignity, present the Church with profound and challenging questions which cannot be lightly evaded. The reservation of the priesthood to males, as a sign of Christ the Spouse who gives himself in the Eucharist, is not a question open to discussion, but it can prove especially divisive if sacramental power is too closely identified with power in general.[31]

The 'power' the Pope speaks about here is defined as the power to administer the Eucharist rather than power in terms of the domination of one person over another. In other words, the power received to administer the Eucharist should not be seen in terms of worldly, hierarchical or sexist power. As a result, women should not view the lack of power to administer the Eucharist as a sign of inferiority. Pope Francis does not specify how women should view it, however.

The words that the priesthood is the reservation of males and 'is not a question open to discussion' are almost lost. However, at the impromptu press conference held aboard the papal plane in July 2013, as Patsy McGarry reports: 'Pope Francis said, "on the ordination of women, the Church has spoken and said no. Pope John Paul II, in a definitive formulation, said that door is closed".'[32] In other words, while the 'feminine genius is needed in all expressions in the life of society', it is not needed in the Church. Yet, in one of his earliest major interviews, as reported by Paddy Agnew, Pope Francis said: 'The church cannot be herself without the woman and her role. The woman is essential for the church. Mary, a woman, is more important than the Bishops ... We must therefore investigate further the role of women in the church.'[33] It seems contradictory to deem women 'essential' for the Church, while at the same time forbidding them to read the gospel at Mass, let alone serve in the ordained ministry of the Church. Yes, you did see that – women are not allowed to read the gospel from the pulpit.

At this point it can be argued that the reasons used and arguments put forward by the Vatican to forbid the ordination of women are tenuous. This, in my view, suggests why John Paul II and Benedict XVI in particular made strong attempts to close down all avenues of discussion. This stance has been successful, as Pope Francis has, as mentioned above, simply said that the 'door is closed' on that particular topic. In other words, the Vatican no longer feels obliged to give a reason as to why women cannot be considered for ordination. Their gender is the reason. In the context of the priesthood, it is all about maleness. To summarise, therefore, the Church Magisterium argues that Jesus deliberately excluded women permanently from taking part in spreading the good news in a leadership capacity.

The above discussion is a basic chronological summary of the arguments against ordaining women. What we are left with is the following: Jesus chose men to follow him, and that choice was to continue in this gender-specific way for all time. However, as the scriptures have proved to be inconclusive, as did the dearth of accounts of the doings of the apostles after Jesus, maleness itself became the focus of new ways of explaining the exclusion of women from the sacrament of ordination. The first weapon used was the fact that Jesus was a man and so only men could represent him. The second was to use nuptial or marital imagery; that is, the Church as bride and Christ as bridegroom. We shall now look at both stances in a little more detail.

REPRESENTATION AND NUPTIAL IMAGERY

The Roman Catholic view is that the priest on the altar represents Christ, and as Christ is a male, only a male can represent him. In *Ordinatio Sacerdotalis*, John Paul II added the following qualification to the choosing of the twelve: 'Also included in this choice were those who, throughout the time of the Church, would carry on the Apostles' mission of representing Christ the Lord and Redeemer.'[34] The use of the words 'representing Christ' is important here. This is because the theological argument used in relation to the impossibility of women as representatives of the divine depends on the literal meaning of the word. Thus the Congregation for the Doctrine of the Faith maintains that a woman cannot preside over the Eucharist because Christ was a man, and only a man can symbolise him properly.

As articulated by the Congregation for the Doctrine of the Faith in the twentieth-century document *Inter Insigniores*, 'we can never ignore the fact that Christ is a man'.[35] This document also talks about the difficulty of seeing Christ in the Eucharist if the celebrant is a woman. Additionally, the *Catechism* explains: 'In the beautiful expression of St Ignatius of Antioch, the bishop is *typos tou Patros*: he is like the living image of God the Father.'[36] In other words, while we are all created in the image and likeness of God, assuming God is male in the human understanding of the word, only men who actually physically resemble a male Christ can represent him, thereby implying that only men can be conduits for the divine. As a result, if we understand the argument literally, women, as per the Catholic Church Magisterium, are in fact *not* created in the image of Christ Jesus.

The Anglican Church, as Archbishop Runcie explained in his communication to John Paul II, teaches that the full humanity of Christ reflects a humanity consisting of male and female, which is why both male and female ministers can reflect the humanity of Christ. In contrast, as explained in *Inter Insigniores*: 'It is true that the priest represents the Church, which is the Body of Christ. But if he does so, it is precisely because he first represents Christ himself.'[37] In other words, first and foremost, the priest represents the male Christ. His representing the Church, made up of the people, is a secondary issue. While change was mooted at the Second Vatican Council to reflect the idea that the priest is in communion with the people rather than set apart from them, in practice this is not the case. The Catholic priest does not represent all of humanity, but rather men alone, as only men can resemble a male Christ. Moreover, when invested with such a distinction, a priest cannot be anything other than 'set apart' from the people.

While the thinking on the male alone representing Christ has a long history, the idea of priest as *repraesentatio Christi* was not actually proposed until the Council of Trent in the sixteenth century. However, it was a proposal that had an authoritative lineage. In the thirteenth century, St Thomas Aquinas, the most influential Church Father, said of women and the sacrament of ordination: 'Accordingly, since it is not possible in the female sex to signify eminence of degree, for a woman is in the state of subjection, it follows that she cannot receive the sacrament of Order.'[38] In other words, women cannot receive the sacrament because they are not only inferior to males but also under male authority and control. Women therefore cannot be leaders. This teaching is so ingrained that, even today, a woman who behaves other than passively or submissively is deemed to be 'unfeminine', as many current cultural values reflect ancient beliefs.

While society is attempting to acknowledge antiquated beliefs and change attitudes towards women, the Church still lags far behind. Aquinas' view about women's 'state of subjection' was reaffirmed in *Inter Insigniores*. The argument about women's lack of physical resemblance to a male Jesus or God is a poor attempt, in my view, to disguise the fact that women's perceived inferiority is at the root of the denial of the sacrament of ordination. The denial of ordination to women, to my mind, comes from the theories and interpretations of mortal men, which are based on thirteenth-century beliefs about women's 'state of subjection'.

There is yet another hurdle to overcome with regard to sexism in the Church and the denial of ordination to women, and that is nuptial imagery: the idea of the Church as the 'bride of Christ' and Christ as the 'bridegroom', represented within the Church by the clergy. Though nuptial imagery has a long history, it is a fairly new stroke in the context of the ordination of women. The New Testament book, Revelation, says: 'Let us rejoice and exult and give him the glory, for the marriage of the Lamb has come, and his bride has made herself ready' (Revelation 19.7). 'Marriage of the Lamb' is a metaphor for the union of Christ as bridegroom and the Church as bride. There are other such examples in Revelation 21.2 and 22.17, as well as in 2 Corinthians 11.2 and Ephesians 5.25–33. In addition, in the Old Testament, there are references to Israel as the bride of God in Isaiah 54.5 and Hosea 2.19–20. These are metaphors for relationships and suggest the close, intertwined bond between Christ and the people of God.

John Paul II argued that this image explained fully both God's relationship to humanity and the specific roles given to men and women by God. It was his inclusion of gender roles, brought into this image in which the topic had no place, that complicated matters. For example, the document *Inter Insigniores* states: 'Christ is the Bridegroom; the Church is his Bride, whom he loves because he has gained her by his blood and made her glorious, holy and without blemish, and henceforth he is inseparable from her.'[39] Here, the death of Jesus and his dying for all is portrayed as a marriage-type relationship. In the Christian context, marriage has definite male and female roles based on natural law theory that encompasses a hierarchical understanding of gender roles. So, while both parties are 'inseparable', the use of the idea of Christian marriage here implies notions of the superiority of one party over another. It also implies a degree of separation between humans and God rather than the teaching, as Jesus said, that the kingdom of God is within human beings.

This concentration on the male gender is again employed in *Mulieris Dignitatem*. John Paul II wrote:

> The Bridegroom – the Son consubstantial with the Father as God – became the son of Mary; he became the "son of man", true man, a male. The symbol of the Bridegroom is masculine. This masculine symbol represents the human aspect of the divine love which God has for Israel, for the Church, and for all people.[40]

The fact of Jesus being the son of Mary is almost lost in the repetition of male-associated terms; 'son', 'father', 'man', 'masculine' and so on. This again echoes the male-centredness of *Inter Insigniores*. John Paul II continued: 'It is the Eucharist that expresses the redemptive act of Christ the Bridegroom towards the Church the Bride. This is clear and unambiguous when the sacramental ministry of the Eucharist, in which the priest acts *in persona Christi*, is performed by a man.'[41] Only a man can be a bridegroom; only a man can enact Jesus dying on the cross for us because Jesus is a man; thus only a man can re-enact this symbolism on the altar. The issue of maleness has never been so emphatic.

There is more. If you think sex is excluded from all of the above, you would be wrong. And despite my well-developed Catholic sense of embarrassment about discussing this topic, I am going to tell you about it anyway. Believe it or not, the male seed is dominant in many aspects of theological discussions. For example, if the representative of Christ on the cross can only be a man, then giving up the body in death becomes an act of coitus, as does, in turn, the symbolic function of the male priest on the altar presiding over the Eucharist. Here is what Cardinal Hans Urs von Balthasar, a member of the Papal Theological Commission, and Pope John Paul II's favourite theological adviser, had to say in 1965. In *Wer ist die Kirche? Vier Skizzen* (*Who is the Church? Four Sketches*), the Cardinal wrote: 'The priestly ministry and the sacrament are means of passing on seed. They are a male preserve. They aim at inducing in the Bride her function as a woman.' Unfortunately, he did not stop there but went on to ask: 'What else is his Eucharist but, at a higher level, an endless act of fruitful outpouring of his whole flesh, such as a man can only achieve for a moment with a limited organ of his body?'[42] In one fell swoop, Christ's death, wherein he identified with human death, is now all about male ejaculation. Sheer mortification prevents me from discussing this further, but I am quite sure readers feel that I do not need to say any more.

Nuptial imagery therefore brings the issue of sexuality into an area in which it has no place. What this imagery does, if one bears in mind Catholic marriage, where two become one – or rather, the woman is subsumed into the identity of the man – is to provide yet another theological-type justification for male authority. As Tina Beattie explains, in this image we are presented with the manliness of Christ, 'whose biological significance is inseparable from his role as Bridegroom and Head of the Church'.[43] In other words, Jesus' male gender becomes central to the topic. There are plenty of other images besides bridegroom used for Christ, such as shepherd, lamb, vine, light and judge. Such images, however, do not assert the authority of man over woman in quite the same useful way.

One of the things *Mulieris Dignitatem* attempted to do was to use Genesis and St Paul's letters to demonstrate that women are present in the idea of the Church as the bride of Christ, and so in that sense, are included. As all, both men and women, are called through the Church to be the bride of Christ, the feminine element is represented. However, the feminine element is not necessarily female, which is why men can be included. Here is how: as all humanity is made up of male and female elements, men can be 'brides'. At the same time, for some reason, women, who are also made up of male and female elements, cannot be 'bridegrooms'. It is therefore another example of a slippery, convoluted argument that attempts to 'explain' something essentially meaningless.

In the eyes of the men of the Church, the woman's role is, first and foremost, that of married motherhood. The woman's task, indeed her vocation, is to care for others. There should be no personal seeking of fulfilment in any guise other than motherhood. That leaves childless women out of the equation: as women who are mothers are seen as secondary from the male hierarchical viewpoint, so women who are childless are considered to be lesser still. In other words, women's value as human beings is still based entirely on their function as procreators: 'woman is the one in whom the order of love in the created world of persons takes first root'.[44] Note the words 'order of love', a phrase coined by St Augustine (354–430) and referred to in *On Christian Marriage: Casti Connubii*, where it is described that in marriage the wife is subject to her husband as he 'is the head of the wife, and Christ is the head of the Church'.[45] This remark explains the quasi-divine status assigned to men over their households in the past. Also, women's 'vocation' to love others selflessly must be conducted in terms of giving up the self. It could, of course, be argued that this is exactly what Jesus did by dying on the cross for humanity, so in this respect, it seems women *can* represent Jesus!

The protracted arguments given for denying the sacrament of ordination to women largely reflect the prejudices against women that have been articulated from the earliest days of Christianity rather than ones based on solid theological justification. Moreover, the thorny issue of gender is essentially, in my view, the 'last resort' argument left to the male hierarchy, and one that infiltrates the various strands of the arguments related to the priesthood being a male preserve. The obsession with human sexuality and the primacy of the male gender has infiltrated so many aspects of theology that it is difficult to stand back from it and question what purpose it serves. At the very least, it forces the issue of gender into every aspect of Catholicism, and subsequently positions women as separate and other. In this model, there is no place for woman as person.

The Church is, after all, ruled by men, with the battle to impose order on it being similar to the often-used idea of the clichéd secular battle between the sexes. I use the word 'battle' deliberately, as the Western culturally-Christian mind-set has positioned male and female in this way, rather than have both genders live harmoniously together, as many do in reality. This battle, or conflict, the Church argues, is a result of Original Sin. This is the biblical theological explanation given for sexual difference and conflict. The Church claims that only through a type of spousal love between man and woman, similar to that of Christ's (bridegroom) love for the Church (bride), will this divide be healed. Spousal love, in Church terms, however, is not exempt from hierarchical notions, and moreover implies the submission of woman to man. Thus balanced, harmonious relationships in which all are valued is a mind-set that is missing from the Catholic context.

ORDINATION THEN AND NOW

Our exploration so far suggests that whatever definition or understanding of leadership roles we have today, whereby only ordained males can celebrate the Eucharist, it was not one shared by the early Christian movement. Moreover, according to St Paul's letters, women do seem to have been accepted by their communities as leaders or ministers in terms of what those roles meant at the time. Students of ancient literature are frequently reminded not to apply modern standards or make judgements on former events. In this context, it seems clear that our understanding of the 'power' of ordination does not appear to bear any resemblance to the appointment of leaders in the early Church movement. As noted earlier, in his apostolic exhortation *Evangelii Gaudium* Pope Francis writes: 'The reservation of the priesthood to males, as a sign of Christ the Spouse who gives himself in the Eucharist, is not a question open to discussion, but it can prove especially divisive if sacramental power is too closely identified with power in general.'[46] The use of the phrase 'sacramental power' is significant here. The interpretation of ordination is that the priest or recipient of the sacrament is invested by the Holy Spirit with the 'power' to celebrate the Eucharist. However, this was not the understanding of ministry in the early Church.

In *The Hidden History of Women's Ordination*, historian and theologian Gary Macy explains that there was a major reform movement in the Church in the eleventh and twelfth centuries. The collection of Church law mentioned earlier, composed by Gratian of Bologna in the twelfth century, included the argument that Jesus would have appointed women to teach if he had thought it proper to do so. To reinforce the point, canonists set out the specialness and distinctiveness of the ordained man from other men. Before this, Macy notes, 'ordination was fundamentally a dedication to a particular role or ministry, not the granting of a special power linked to the liturgy of the altar'.[47] This ties in with St Paul's letters and his greetings to the various people, men and women, in the communities he had established. Not until the Third and Fourth Lateran Councils (taking place in 1179 and 1215, respectively), therefore, did the idea take hold that a spiritual power was received in ordination. Before that time, and as we shall see in the next chapter, men and women, married and single, carried out various functions in Christian communities, including celebrating the Eucharist.[48]

In the wake of these councils, it was decided that the women in the scriptures and in Paul's letters were not properly ordained and were therefore an aberration. This was a logical decision at the time, as women, being 'misbegotten' or 'defective' males, 'deficient in reason' and in the 'status of subjection', to use a few descriptive phrases applied to them, could not possibly be leaders or teachers. In this context, they should not have been in leadership roles because of their gender: the 'impediment of sex'. As Macy writes: 'Henceforth, only the ceremony empowering a priest or deacon would be a true ordination, and anything called an ordination in the past that was not an ordination to the priesthood or diaconate was not an ordination.'[49]

Thus, today, the priesthood, as it is understood by the Church, is absolutely bound up with the male gender. As it stands, the Catholic Church's understanding of the nature of the priesthood would have to be completely altered to facilitate women's ministry. The male is the living image of Christ and thus only he can celebrate the Eucharist. Only he is invested with that 'power'. Yet, if all human beings are created in the image and likeness of God, how are we to understand these arguments? Furthermore, as we shall see in the next chapter, the scriptures confirm that women did accompany Jesus, they witnessed his death and resurrection, they served in leadership roles in the early Church and they worked alongside St Paul in his apostolic work as well as in the communities he established. Is the Church saying, therefore, that Paul got it all wrong?

4

WHAT ABOUT THE WOMEN?

'IN THE IMAGE OF GOD HE CREATED THEM'

> So God created humankind in his image, in the image of God he created them; male and female he created them. (Genesis 1.27)

The terms 'male and female' indicate, the *HarperCollins Study Bible* explains, that '[b]oth man and woman are created in the image of God, who is beyond gender or comprises both'.[1] This is not a recent revelation. For example, the great mystic Julian of Norwich (1342–1416) wrote in *Revelations of Divine Love*: 'And thus I saw that God rejoices that he is our Father; God rejoices that he is our mother.'[2] Mysticism is the experience of direct access to God. Another mystic and doctor of the Church, Catherine of Siena (1347–80), wrote that Jesus told her: 'With me there is no male or female.'[3] In the mystical context, the Doctrine of Synderesis (or Synteresis) understands that a divine spark exists in every human being. It is highly unlikely that this divine spark has limitations attached to it based on the gender of the recipient. Yet, for thousands of years, everything from the scriptures to art and discourse has taught us that God is exclusively male, despite the message that all humans are created 'in the image of God'.

In short, not only is the female voice missing from the Church, so too is the female divine. If we are lucky enough to have a father and a mother, we can appreciate the value of both. Both respond to and take care of the different needs we have at various times. In my view, this explains why devotion to Our Lady is so important to so many, as she is, to all intents and purposes, the feminine divine for Catholics. However, she is not God. This lack of acknowledgement for the female divine is something that women in other organised religions are recognising, while an awareness of how the scriptures have been used to position women as lesser is also being realised.[4]

Julian, in her vision of God as mother and father, was inadvertently questioning the interpretation reached in *Decretum Gratiani*, the twelfth-century collection of Canon Laws mentioned earlier, that women were not in fact created in the image of God. How could they be, given their gendered defects? Women were inferior to men simply because they were women. They could not, therefore, be considered spiritual equals – they needed a male to intercede for them, a male to guide them and a male to be in charge of them. This mind-set is at the heart of women's position on the periphery, but to date has not been acknowledged or confronted.

As we have seen, women are 'reassured' time and again that they hold a 'special position' in the Catholic Church. However, it is difficult to understand what this phrase actually means in a context where, first, the Church hierarchy continues to deny the share in the divinity that women have;

and second, to position them as having less of a spiritual capacity than men. One cannot promulgate teaching on the 'special position' of women in the Catholic Church while at the same time teaching that women cannot be called to serve in an official capacity by the Holy Spirit. Furthermore, how are women supposed to process their 'special position' status in a Church that teaches that, on the one hand, human beings are all created in the image and likeness of God, but on the other, to actually represent that God, one has to be a man, because God is a man? In other words, in the Catholic institutional worldview, women are *not* created in the image of God. Somehow or other, women are supposed to accept that the spirit that is within all of us does not quite cut the mustard when it resides in a female body, and that the divine aspect of self that is present in everyone – that is, our souls – is somehow different in women. Thus, if there is no divine feminine in God, that leaves nothing in the divine realm with which women can identify.

Jesus' good news for all was to assure humankind that every person is of equal value to God. Every person has a soul, a spark of divinity. There is no hierarchy. There is no divine 'order'. Given the Church's focus on men and male-ness, it is worth returning to the gospels and St Paul's letters to refocus our attention on women, who were, you will be reassured to know, very much present in the early movement and in the early Church. As it is the actions of Jesus that are cited as stumbling blocks to the inclusion of women, as well as the importance given to the idea that the tradition of the Church is to emulate the actions of Jesus, the next step to consider is how clear Jesus was about excluding women from actively engaging in his mission, and furthermore, if his interaction with women supports their secondary status in the eyes of the institutional Church. We shall now explore that question by looking at women in the gospel accounts in the order they were composed: Mark, Matthew, Luke and John.

WOMEN IN THE GOSPELS

Finding detailed accounts of women in the gospels is not an easy task. As with most accounts in history (which is not called *his-story* for nothing), the focus is on the doings of males, with females included mainly in terms of their relationships to particular men. While the authors of the gospels may not have set out intentionally to under-represent women in their respective accounts, it is not unusual for cultural norms that saw women as insignificant and inferior to emerge in early Christian writings. Writers reflect what is happening around them and the various gospels either responded to or reflected the contemporary situation of the emerging Christian movement. The synoptic gospels usually have the same incidents, described in similar ways, which either differ in John's much later account or are not mentioned at all. Additionally, Luke's account is, as noted earlier, a fleshed-out 'biography' of Jesus in comparison to the factual style of the gospels of Mark and Matthew.

The first woman mentioned in the gospels is Simon Peter's mother-in-law, whom Jesus cured of illness. She appears in the gospels of Mark, Matthew and Luke, but is not mentioned in John's account (Mark 1.30–31; Matthew 8.14–15; Luke 4.38–39). Thus, Simon Peter, who was the first person

Jesus called upon to follow him, had a mother-in-law, and therefore also a wife. Simon Peter, whom, we are taught, the Bishop of Rome/pope succeeds, therefore was not celibate. We shall return to this topic later.

There are many accounts of Jesus curing illness in various women throughout the gospels, such as the woman suffering from haemorrhages who touches the hem of Jesus' cloak. This incident is described only in the synoptic gospels. Then there is a woman who asks Jesus to help her daughter, who has 'an unclean spirit'. She is of Syrophoenician origin in Mark, but a Canaanite in Matthew, and she and her daughter become a father and son in Luke's account (Mark 7.24; Matthew 15.21–28; Luke 9.37–43). Already, we can see how details can change between the different accounts.

The famous story of the anointing of Jesus with oil is particularly interesting in this regard. In Mark's and Matthew's accounts, the nameless woman of Bethany anoints Jesus' head with costly oil. Jesus defends her actions when his companions complain: 'Truly, I tell you, wherever the good news is proclaimed in the whole world, what she has done will be told in remembrance of her' (Mark 14.3–9; Matthew 26.6–13). Sadly, this has not been the case because we have not been given her name. Moreover, by the time we get to Luke's gospel, this woman is described as a 'sinful woman' who washes Jesus' feet with her tears, anoints them with oil and dries them with her hair (Luke 7.36–50). In John's gospel, her transformation is even more extreme, as she becomes Mary, of Martha and Mary fame, who anoints Jesus' feet with perfume and then wipes them with her hair (John 12.1–8). As well as showing how women can be 'blended' into one another, the story serves as a useful example of how difficult it is to verify, for want of a better word, specific accounts of events in the New Testament.

Let us look at a few more examples. Matthew specifies 'women and children' among the crowds who follow Jesus (see, for example, Matthew 15.38). In Luke's story too there are women present among Jesus' followers. We are not told whether the women among Jesus' followers were called by him or simply decided to follow him. Notably, Jesus does not send them away. Indeed, at one point he says, 'anyone who comes to me I will never drive away' (John 6.37). However, the reassertion of cultural norms is apparent in John's gospel, as women rarely appear and they are not mentioned as being among Jesus' followers. Indeed, his disciples express their astonishment when Jesus converses with the Samaritan woman he meets at the well, a story that appears only in John's gospel (John 4.7–42). There are two things of note in this incident. First, it was against the social customs of the time for Jesus, as a Jewish teacher, to speak with a woman in public. That he does so suggests that Jesus deliberately broke the barriers of gender and race that were in existence at the time. Second, we are told: 'Many Samaritans from that city believed in him because of the woman's testimony' (John 4.39). In other words, Jesus deliberately chose to speak to this woman so that she would testify to the community that he was the Messiah. If Jesus' actions of deliberately choosing men as apostles is significant, then significance can also be given to this event: women could be witnesses and could spread the good news.

The famous story of the woman tried for committing

adultery is related only in John's gospel (John 8.1–11). The man she commits adultery with is neither charged nor mentioned; and as was culturally the norm, the woman alone is to be stoned. Yet Jesus does not condemn her: 'Let anyone among you who is without sin be the first to throw a stone at her' (John 8.7). He, no doubt, appreciated that this woman did not commit adultery alone. Interestingly, most scholars now agree that this story was inserted into John's gospel at a later date and was not in the earlier versions. We can only speculate about why this was done, as the deliberate insertion of the story suggests an author with an agenda. It is likely that the author was attempting to show the magnanimity of Jesus by choosing an example of what he had decided was the most serious sin he could think of for Jesus to forgive.

The deliberate insertion of the story into John's gospel, thereby giving it both credence and authority, suggests how soon after the death of Jesus cultural norms were reasserted. In other words, accounts of women in the gospel stories were already being manipulated to suit perceived notions of women's inferior status in society, as well as the belief in women's tendency to sin in the sexual arena unless strictly monitored. At the same time, other stories about Jesus' interactions with women, such as the woman at the well, were not, in my view, given the same consideration as those told about the males he encountered. His defence of the women he interacted with, in the face of criticism from his disciples and others, serves as an example of how all humans are equal in the eyes of God. It is difficult to grasp what the modern Church's motive is for retaining the story of the adulterous woman, which is still read aloud at Mass, despite what is now known about its composition. Perhaps the institution is reluctant to give up such a useful example of a truly benevolent Lord, whose mercy towards such a lowly creature shows his love for all sinners despite their flaws, although, in my view, the story of Peter denying Jesus three times is a more useful example of Jesus' forgiveness.

The account in which women feature most significantly in the gospels is in the descriptions of the crucifixion and resurrection of Jesus. Notably, the disciples are not present at the crucifixion scenes as, just as Jesus had foretold, and as recounted in Mark's and Matthew's gospels, they had deserted him. Matthew wrote that Jesus told his disciples before his arrest that they would desert him: 'You will all become deserters because of me this night' (Matthew 26.31). After his arrest, Jesus' words are validated: 'Then all of the disciples deserted him and fled' (Matthew 26.56). Similarly, Mark wrote: '[A]ll of them deserted him and fled' (Mark 14.50). It seems certain, therefore, that the disciples were not present at one of the defining moments of Christian orthodoxy: the crucifixion. Additionally, it has to be pointed out that despite this, their characters have not been vilified for centuries for their desertion of Jesus. All of the gospels tell of the women witnessing the crucifixion, but the popular image of women at the foot of the cross occurs only in John's account. In the synoptic gospels, the women observe the events from a distance.

We shall look at the descriptions of these important scenes in order of composition, taking note of the differences between them. Mark described the scene as follows:

> There were also women looking on from a distance; among them were Mary Magdalene, and Mary the mother of James the younger and of Joses, and Salome. These used to follow him and provided for him when he was in Galilee; and there were many other women who had come up with him to Jerusalem. (Mark 15.40–41)

In this piece, therefore, it appears that women accompanied Jesus on his travels as followers. Similarly, Matthew wrote:

> Many women were also there, looking on from a distance; they had followed Jesus from Galilee and had provided for him. Among them were Mary Magdalene, and Mary the mother of James and Joseph, and the mother of the sons of Zebedee. (Matthew 27.55–56)

The wording here is very similar to Mark's account. Luke, who does not name the women, simply wrote: 'But all his acquaintances, including the women who had followed him from Galilee, stood at a distance, watching these things' (Luke 23.49). John was equally succinct: 'Meanwhile, standing near the cross of Jesus were his mother, and his mother's sister, Mary the wife of Clopas, and Mary Magdalene' (John 19.25).

Mary Magdalene is the only woman specifically named in three of the accounts, so we can be certain that she was there. There is little doubt, too, about the presence of women at the crucifixion and of them being among Jesus' followers. However, women as followers of Jesus did not sit well with later Church luminaries, so one way to downplay their role was to diminish their status. This was done by focusing on the words used in relation to the women in Mark's and Matthew's accounts: 'provided for him'. The meaning was taken literally and was understood to mean that the women present among his followers were simply looking after Jesus, either financially or as nurturers and carers. Thus, the Church argues, they were not there because of the appeal of his words and deeds, but simply to look after him. In this way women are positioned in their usual role of appendages to the males among Jesus' followers, which would have been a more acceptable position for them in the eyes of the Church. However, it is significant that Mary Magdalene does not appear to be attached to any man, in contrast to the other women mentioned. As a result, she is a particular target for Church writers who, as we shall see, manipulate her representation beyond all recognition.

In the next scene, Jesus' body has been removed from the cross and brought to the tomb. Mark wrote: 'Mary Magdalene and Mary the mother of Joses saw where the body was laid' (Mark 15.47). Similarly, Matthew wrote: 'Mary Magdalene and the other Mary were there, sitting opposite the tomb' (Matthew 27.61). It is not certain who 'the other Mary' is in this case. Luke does not name the women who were at the tomb: 'The women who had come with him from Galilee followed, and they saw the tomb and how his body was laid. Then they returned, and prepared spices and ointments' (Luke 23.55–56). Finally, in John's account there is no mention of women going to the tomb until the morning of the resurrection; bearing in mind that his is the latest account, we can surmise that, at this point, women are already being cut from the story.

It becomes more difficult to erase women from the next scene as they are highly visible in the accounts of the resurrection of Jesus. In Mark's account, it is Mary Magdalene, Mary the mother of James, and Salome who go to the tomb. A young man in a white robe tells them that Jesus has risen and commands: 'But go, tell his disciples and Peter that he is going ahead of you to Galilee; there you will see him, just as he told you' (Mark 16.7). There are two endings to Mark's gospel, which appear to have been composed at different times. In the longer ending, believed to be the earlier version, Jesus appears to Mary Magdalene before appearing to the disciples: 'Now after he rose early on the first day of the week, he appeared first to Mary Magdalene' (Mark 16.9).

In Matthew's account, it is Mary Magdalene and 'the other Mary' who go to the tomb (Matthew 28.1). As I said, the identity of this 'other Mary' is not specified, so we cannot be certain that she is Jesus' mother. In Matthew's account, the young man is now described as an angel who removes the stone and shows the women the empty tomb. He instructs them to tell the disciples that Jesus 'has been raised from the dead' (Matthew 28.7). On their way to the house where the disciples have gathered, Jesus appears to both women: 'Suddenly Jesus met them and said, "Greetings!" And they came to him, took hold of his feet, and worshipped him. Then Jesus said to them, "Do not be afraid; go and tell my brothers to go to Galilee; there they will see me"' (Matthew 28.9–10).

Details begin to change when we get to the next two accounts. In Luke's account, the women who go to the tomb and see that it is empty are initially not named. Moreover, the lone man or angel who appears to tell the women that Jesus has risen becomes *two* men, who are later identified as angels (Luke 24.23). The unnamed women tell their story and the narrator remarks: 'Now it was Mary Magdalene, Joanna, Mary the mother of James, and the other women with them who told this to the apostles' (Luke 24.10–11). The reception of this news by the apostles is also described and we are told that they are sceptical, as similarly mentioned in Mark's account. Indeed, Peter goes to the tomb to check on the women's story. In addition, Luke's gospel includes an extra tale at this point. Two disciples, one called Cleopas, are talking about the empty tomb on their way to a village called Emmaus when Jesus appears to them. They do not realise who he is and urge the stranger to accompany them and eat with them. This Jesus does: 'When he was at the table with them, he took bread, blessed and broke it, and gave it to them. Then their eyes were opened, and they recognised him; and he vanished from their sight' (Luke 24.30–31). The men journey on to Jerusalem where they visit the eleven disciples and, as Luke writes: 'They were saying, "The Lord has risen indeed, and he has appeared to Simon!"' (Luke 24.34). However, this scene of Jesus appearing to Simon Peter is not described.

Finally, in John's account, Mary Magdalene goes to the tomb by herself and finds it empty. She runs off to get Simon Peter and 'the disciple Jesus loved', who return with her to the tomb. Mary Magdalene remains at the tomb while the disciples return to the others. Then two angels appear to her, and while she is telling them why she is weeping, Jesus appears and says to her:

'Do not hold on to me, because I have not yet ascended to the Father. But go to my brothers and say to them, "I am ascending to my Father and your Father, to my God and your God".' Mary Magdalene went and announced to the disciples, 'I have seen the Lord'; and she told them that he had said these things to her. (John 20.17–18)

It appears from Jesus' words that he is telling Mary Magdalene that their time together is at an end. His mission on earth is fulfilled but she must go and tell the disciples that she has seen the risen Jesus. His words to her are quite poignant. The particular translation above is closest to the original Greek. The Latin translation in *The New Jerusalem Bible* is terser: 'Do not cling to me', which suggests the cliché of a clingy woman holding up the hero from his important mission.[5]

While some modern urban legends suggest that Jesus and Mary Magdalene were married, there is no evidence in the Bible for this. At the same time, in the Gnostic Gospel of Philip there is a passage that suggests a close relationship between them:

the companion of the [Savior is] Mary Magdalene. [But Christ loved] her more than [all] the disciples, and used to kiss her [often] on her [mouth]. The rest of [the disciples were offended] … They said to him, 'Why do you love her more than all of us?' The Savior answered and said to them, 'Why do I not love you as [I love] her?'[6]

Jesus' answer suggests that the disciples do not quite measure up to Mary in his estimation! In any case, there appears to be a strong bond between them as Jesus prepares Mary Magdalene for their upcoming separation. This is important, as the affection Jesus shows towards Mary Magdalene and the responsibility he gives her by asking her to repeat the account of his resurrection to the eleven, cannot be overlooked. It is clear that not only does he value her as he does the male disciples, but more than that, he entrusts her with the mission of recounting the story of his resurrection. Notable also is the fact that it was Jesus' female followers who provided the testimony for his suffering, death and resurrection. It was his women followers who witnessed these events and who told others about what had happened. They are therefore witnesses – a role, as we saw earlier, that was gradually imbued with specific authority.

While details among the accounts differ, there are some elements that remain consistent. First, Mary Magdalene was one of Jesus' followers and was present at the crucifixion. She witnessed the resurrection, and the resurrected Jesus told her to proclaim the message to the disciples that, through his victory over death, everlasting life was a promise for those who believed. There is no doubt that this is a powerful mission entrusted to her by Jesus. Moreover, this promise is a central tenet of Christianity. The *Catholic Dictionary* defines the resurrection as follows: 'A basic truth of the Christian Faith and an essential part of the teaching of the Church from the earliest days.' It is also 'the model for the bodily resurrection of all the faithful on the last day'. This 'basic truth' was witnessed by Mary Magdalene, who was told personally by Jesus to recount what had happened.

Whatever the anomalies are between the various accounts of the crucifixion and resurrection described above, we can be pretty certain that it was Jesus' women followers who witnessed his death and were responsible for relating the story of his suffering, death and resurrection. If you are surprised by this revelation, here is the reason why: as we have just seen, the resurrected Jesus appears to Mary Magdalene in three of the four accounts. Yet, as discussed earlier, it is Luke's account in which Jesus is said to have appeared to Simon Peter first that is invoked by the teaching authority of the Church. This single account of Jesus appearing first to Simon Peter, a male, is deemed to be more authentic than the three versions recounting that the risen Jesus first appeared to a woman. In other words, Simon Peter's relating of the events, as told to him by Jesus' female followers, was invested with authenticity and authority. As a result, Peter is deemed to be the rightful leader of the Church. However, as, logically, three accounts outweigh one, it is Mary Magdalene as first witness of the resurrection who should have that distinction.

The implications of Mary Magdalene's role in the gospel story have not been confronted by the Church. Given her role in the resurrection and her presence throughout the key events of Jesus' life, death and resurrection, is she any different from the male disciples and apostles? But rather than accept her as an equal to the male disciples, the disparagement of her character was undertaken by eminent Christian writers from the sixth century onwards, so that her role reflected their particular worldviews. The remodelling of the representation of Mary Magdalene will be discussed in more detail later.

If Jesus' actions in relation to choosing the twelve are considered to be deliberate, then the following questions arise: was it a deliberate act by Jesus to choose women to witness his crucifixion and death? If so, what are the implications of the exclusion of men from this scene, given that so much fuss is made about women's supposed absence from the Last Supper? Moreover, was Mary Magdalene an apostle – the leader of the women followers? To explore some of these questions, we shall now look to the early Church as a way of learning how the earliest followers of Jesus might have interpreted his teachings and example.

WOMEN IN THE LETTERS OF ST PAUL

Outside the gospels, accounts of women in the early Christian movement can be found in the letters of St Paul, to which we shall now turn. These letters, composed before the gospels, are the earliest written accounts of the 'Jesus movement'. The letters of St Paul give us clues about the people he worked with and the communities he established. The letters were written over a period of about ten years, some twenty years after the death of Jesus. Despite being written before the gospels, they, in a similar vein to Acts, focus on the period after the death of Jesus. It is interesting to note that the writings of St Paul indicate that women ministered alongside him, as they are named in his letters. Moreover, the tone of these letters suggests Paul's high regard for his colleagues, both male and female, who dedicated themselves to working for the Lord and for the community.

Paul's letters to the communities he founded contain a vivid account of the teachings of the Christian faith. Much

debate has centred on the authenticity of these letters, and
the consensus is that Romans, 1 Corinthians, 2 Corinthians,
Galatians, Philippians, 1 Thessalonians and Philemon are
genuine Pauline letters, while there is some lingering argument over the authorship of Ephesians, Colossians and 2
Thessalonians. It is extremely doubtful that Paul wrote 1
Timothy, 2 Timothy and Titus, as they appear to be later
works and have stylistic and syntactical differences from
the authentic letters. In addition, Hebrews was erroneously
attributed to Paul. Finally, Acts of the Apostles, which
recounts the establishment of early Christian communities
and is thought to be a later work written by the person who
also composed the Gospel of Luke, differs in many details
from the accounts in Paul's letters. Therefore, the accounts
in Paul's letters are probably the most reliable source for his
mission.

The order of the authenticated letters is thought to be
roughly as follows: 1 Thessalonians (AD 50–51); Galatians
(AD 50–56); 1 Corinthians (AD 54); Philemon (AD 55–59);
2 Corinthians (AD 55–56); Philippians (AD 55–65); and
Romans (AD 56–57).

Paul's first letter to the Corinthians opens with a call to
unity based on faith and baptism, and he responds to several
matters of dispute raised by the believers in Corinth. The
large number of stories and interpretations circulating after
the death of Jesus about his life, death and teachings, as discussed in Chapter One, is reflected by Paul's concern with
the possibility of false teachings. He mentions that 'Chloe's
people' have told him about various quarrels (1 Corinthians
1.11). It seems likely that Chloe was a prominent Christian

woman in the community in Corinth. In both of Paul's letters to the Corinthians, which scholars posit are likely to be a composite of up to five letters, he expresses his concern about the community's susceptibility to false apostles, whom he terms 'super-apostles' (2 Corinthians 11.5; 12.11).

His letter to the Philippians expresses similar concerns about false prophets. In light of these 'enemies of the cross of Christ', Paul urges the community to 'stand firm in the Lord' (Philippians 4.1). He then turns his attention to two women, Euodia and Syntyche:

> I urge Euodia and I urge Syntyche to be of the same mind in the Lord. Yes, and I ask you also, my loyal companion, help these women, for they have struggled beside me in the work of the gospel, together with Clement and the rest of my co-workers, whose names are in the book of life. (Philippians 4.2–3)

It appears that Euodia and Syntyche had diverse understandings about some aspects of either practice or teaching. Paul appeals to them directly, which implies their importance in the movement, and moreover urges the community to help them as 'they have struggled beside me in the work of the gospel'. Paul's use of the words 'beside me' conveys the women's equal status, in his worldview, in terms of their work for the Lord.

There are a notable number of women included in the greetings in Paul's letters. What is also of interest is how he describes these women. His greetings suggest that, first, the named women were very much part of the early Christian movement, and second, that they held various types of leadership roles. In Romans, which is thought to be the last of Paul's letters, he wrote (I have indicated female names in bold):

> I commend to you our sister **Phoebe**, a deacon of the church at Cenchrease, so that you may welcome her in the Lord as is fitting for the saints, and help her in whatever she may require from you, for she has been a benefactor of many and of myself as well. Greet **Prisca** and Aquila, who work with me in Christ Jesus ... Greet **Mary**, who has worked very hard among you. Greet Andronicus and **Junia** ... they are prominent among the apostles, and they were in Christ before I was ... Greet those workers in the Lord, **Tryphaena** and **Tryphosa** ... Greet Rufus, chosen in the Lord: and greet **his mother** – a mother to me also. Greet ... **Julia**, Nereus and his **sister** ... and all the saints who are with them. (Romans 16.1–15)

Among the people greeted in the passage above are a married couple, Prisca (1 Corinthians 16.19; called Priscilla in Romans 16.3–4) and her husband Aquila (Acts 18.1; 1 Corinthians 16.19). Thus both men and women, married and single, are heads of individual house churches or very much involved in working with Paul. Marital status is not an issue, nor is gender. Moreover, in this extract, Paul is clearly telling the community that Phoebe is his emissary. Paul had been working on his mission for about twenty years at this point. While the word 'deacon' is used in relation to Phoebe here, the *HarperCollins Study Bible* explains that terms for various ranks of authority had not been coined; however, the word indicates some form of recognised leadership role. We can infer that Phoebe is representing Paul in whatever he might have done himself in Rome – preaching, teaching and solving disputes – and thus her status in Paul's eyes is one of authority. It can be argued, therefore, that the women mentioned here, in a similar vein to Paul, felt called to spread the faith and are 'workers in the Lord'. If that call came from the Holy Spirit, as is the case when recounted in Acts, why is it assumed by the contemporary Church that the Holy Spirit no longer calls women to serve?

An interesting detail recorded in Romans is the fact that Junia is female. However, there is evidence that by the late Middle Ages this name had been translated in the scriptures to the male form, Junias. This is significant because Junia is described, along with her male colleague Andronicus, as being 'prominent among the apostles'. Whether she and Andronicus are actual apostles, worked with the apostles or were known by the apostles is still disputed by scholars. However, the revision of her name shows how easily the elimination of the female from the Christian story was achieved. Prominent Christian writers, from the fifth century onwards, appear to have taken it for granted that women could not have held leadership roles in the early Church.

There is another interesting story in relation to Paul. The Acts of Paul and Thecla is among the body of Apocryphal writings.[7] In contrast to the New Testament works, women's roles as disciples are defined in these accounts, rather than merely being hinted at. The story of Thecla is one such account. Thecla was a young woman who defied convention by refusing to marry the wealthy suitor chosen for her by her family. She heard Paul speak when he visited her village and vowed to join him on his mission. This was a radical step for a young woman who was duty-bound to marry and have children. Despite intense opposition from her family and community, she joined him and he sent her out on her own to preach, saying: 'Go and teach the word of God!'. She did so until her eventual martyrdom.[8] Thecla's story is a tale of adversity and adventure, which shares many traits with Ancient Greek novels, though her story has a definite religious purpose. She proves her worth and her capability to teach the word of God by overcoming suffering and adversity. The story ends as follows: '[A]fter enlightening many with the word of God she slept with a noble sleep.'[9]

It is impossible to determine whether Thecla actually existed, but it is the fact of the preservation of the story from the time of its composition, thought to be in the mid-second century, up to the Second Vatican Council (1962–65), when Thecla was dropped from the list of saints, that is significant. In other words, the story of a woman answering the call to serve God was passed on from generation to generation. Moreover, the story must have been in circulation for some time before being written down. While we do not know if the story was told as an exceptional case, or simply as part of the early Christian story that saw women preach and teach until Church councils forbade them to do so, it does suggest that the idea of women preaching and teaching was not inconceivable.

There are other points of note in Thecla's story. She, in a similar vein to Paul, felt called to spread the good news and simply did so, which indicates that 'the call' is not gender-specific. She, too, like many of the apostles, was captured, imprisoned and persecuted. Another element of her story is her association with virginity, a topic to which we shall return later. Like Paul, she favoured celibacy for herself. However, when she is discussed by Christian writers from the fourth century onwards, who we will look at more closely in the next chapter, it is her virginity rather than her ministry that is emphasised. These writers promoted the idea that celibacy was one way for women to redeem themselves from the sins of Eve. Thus, by moulding Thecla's story to suit the male perspective, she became the model for the women who felt called to serve God as virgins rather than as teachers. As Mary T. Malone writes, 'from the end of the second century, it is only virgins who break through the universal Christian silence about women'.[10]

As my explorations show, women had leadership roles in the early stages of the Christian movement. At the Council of Nicaea (325), deaconesses were removed from the orders of the clergy, a prohibition which in itself suggests that deaconesses were active up to that time. As this veto had to be repeated at a series of councils and synods, such as Laodicea (363), Nimes (394) and Orange (441), it seems that women continued to minister until at least the fifth century, despite the series of edicts banning them from doing so. Indeed, there are indications that the practice may have continued for even longer than that. For example, the Wijngaards Institute for Catholic Research notes that Canon 73 of the Synod of Worms, held in Germany in 868, reads as follows:

No woman should be ordained before she is forty years old and then with great discretion. If, however, after receiving the laying on of hands and having stayed for some time in the ministry, she then gives herself over to marriage, she will be excommunicated because she has put shame on God's grace ... as also the man who is joined to her.[11]

This would suggest that there were women deacons functioning in the ninth century. Thus the 'tradition' that women did not play a part in Church leadership, or that they did not work to spread the good news, or indeed have roles in early Christian communities, is certainly not the case. Moreover, it seems clear that the early Christian movement did not practise the permanent male-only, priest-type role that was later promoted as having been established by Jesus as a perennial norm.

As the story of Jesus' life and mission demonstrates, women were not only a visible presence but were also included in his vision for the world. For the men of the early Catholic Church, however, women were a puzzle, a danger, an inconvenience and an unnecessary element to the organisational development and sustainability of Christianity. As a result, much time and effort was spent on fitting the women in the Bible into the cultural mind-set of the time. Our Lady and Mary Magdalene were of particular interest and, as we shall see, the manipulation of their stories by Christian writers is useful for gaining an insight into how deliberately the exclusion of women from ministry was undertaken and maintained.

5

THE FALL OF WOMEN IN THE CATHOLIC CHURCH

THE CHURCH FATHERS

Given the evidence in relation to women's roles in the burgeoning early Christian movement, the next question we need to ask is why women are not welcome in leadership roles in the Church of today? How were women erased from the Christian story? As we have seen, Jesus mixed freely, spoke with and defended women throughout his ministry. They were included among his followers and they testified to his ministry. However, as little as fifty years after the time of Jesus, such inclusiveness had begun to be overturned. While in one sense the suppression of women's roles in the new religion was gradual, the most decisive activity on the positioning of women as inferior and subordinate to men occurred as a result of the late-fourth- and early-fifth-century writings of a body of men known as the Fathers of the Church.

The *Catholic Dictionary* explains that this designation:

> was given to writers of the early Church, many of whom were also bishops; originally a mark of respect accorded only

to heads of churches as indicative of their responsibility for discipline and doctrine within the family of the Church as the human father is in his family; later extended more broadly to those notable for the orthodoxy of their doctrine, who by their writing, preaching, and holy lives defended the Faith.

These men, who are declared by this description as being in charge of all the faithful, just as a father is in charge of his family, wrote extensively, among other topics, about celibacy and sexuality. There are many more writers than those discussed briefly below, as the extraordinary body of material written, often in torturous detail, about celibacy, the body and the evils of sexuality, in particular female sexuality, is sizeable.

The Latin Church embraced the worldview of the Roman Empire with its enthusiasm for laws, penalties and hierarchical organisation. It was from this mind-set, which viewed women as being secondary, that the influential Church Fathers emerged. It is important to bear in mind that the starting point for these writers with regard to women was that women were unquestionably inferior to men. Thus, while women played a pivotal role in the musings of the Fathers of the Church, those musings were dominated by a negative, misguided and often misogynist point of view about women that proved detrimental to the perception of women across the Christian world.

The most influential of these writers were Ambrose (*c.* 339–97), who served as Bishop of Milan from 374 until his death; Jerome, the biblical theologian of Rome who, as mentioned earlier, translated the Bible into Latin; and Augustine, the North African Bishop of Hippo. Later, the work of Thomas Aquinas in the Middle Ages would also shape Christianity and provide a lasting legacy of negativity regarding the human body.

Given the contemporary cultural context that saw women as inferior beings, the roles played by Mary the mother of Jesus and Mary Magdalene proved particularly troublesome for the Fathers of the Church. How could a mere woman be mother of the Saviour, and a second one, Mary Magdalene, be his close companion? As a result of this dilemma, much time and effort was expended in squaring the representation of these women in the Bible story to what was acceptable in the minds of the Fathers of the Church. To this end, Mary the mother of Jesus and Mary Magdalene were 'moulded' to suit contemporary views about women.

MARY AND MARY MAGDALENE

Mary the mother of Jesus is less visible in the various gospel accounts than one might expect, given her status in the later Church. In the earliest of the gospels, that of Mark, Mary listens, with the crowd, to her adult son speak (Mark 3.31–35). This story is repeated in Matthew and Luke (8.19), with some small differences, although all of the synoptic gospels mention that Mary was accompanied by Jesus' siblings (Matthew 13.46). In Luke, she also appears in the well-known story about going to see the twelve-year-old Jesus speak in the Temple (Luke 2.41–51).

Jesus' birth is not described at all in Mark, as in that account he first appears as an adult being baptised by John. Matthew provides only a short account of Jesus' birth where we are simply told that he was born of Mary, although the angel appears to Joseph to tell him what will happen.

In Luke's gospel, this angel first appears to the husband of Elizabeth, Mary's cousin, to foretell the birth of John the Baptist. The angel then appears to Mary and tells her that she will give birth to the Saviour. The famous nativity scene is also presented in Luke's gospel, probably because, as mentioned earlier, this is an expanded account of Jesus' life. As a literary text, therefore, a lengthy description of Jesus' origins and early life would be expected. As a result, Luke is the only one who tells us of Jesus' childhood in Nazareth, of his being brought to the Temple as an infant and of his preaching there at the age of twelve. In John's gospel, and in a similar vein to Mark's account, Jesus is introduced as an adult who is baptised by John the Baptist, an event that all the gospels relate. Finally, in John's account, Mary the mother of Jesus appears at the wedding feast at Cana, a story that does not appear in the other gospels.

From this brief overview, Mary, who serves as the ideological example of virtue and Christian motherhood we know today, is one shaped from quite slim pickings. To be the mother of Jesus was not enough in itself for the Church Fathers, as Mary was, in their worldview, a lowly woman. As a result, Mary had to be invested with other virtues to justify giving her the status suitable for the important role of mother of the Saviour. It can be argued that the whole point of Jesus being born of woman was to underline his identification with humanity. However, prevailing views on women meant that the men of the Church could not accept that an ordinary woman could assume this role. Additionally, at this point in Christianity – the fourth century – sex was regarded as a sin, yet Mary, as the mother of Jesus, could not be a sinner or, therefore, a sexual being. As a result, the human Mary, who had given birth to Jesus in the usual manner, could not be countenanced. Thus began what can only be called the obsession with the physical aspect of Mary's motherhood and the idea of her virginity remaining intact for her entire life.

One major dilemma for the Church Fathers was how to accommodate the fact that Jesus appeared to have siblings, as this indicated that Mary *was* a sexual being. While Jesus was spiritually 'placed' in Mary's womb, her other children were not, so how could this be acceptable in terms of Mary as virgin? As mentioned earlier, the synoptic gospels refer to Jesus' siblings (Mark 6.3, Matthew 13.46, Luke 8.19). And, according to Acts of the Apostles, Jesus' brother James, who was martyred some time prior to the Jewish War of AD 66–79, was one of the key leaders of the Church in Jerusalem (Acts 15.13; 21.18). James is referred to by Paul as 'James the Lord's brother' (Galatians 1.18), which makes his relationship to Jesus difficult to dispute. However, the Church Fathers were not deterred.

One solution to the quest to establish Mary's purity was to pass Jesus' siblings off as children of Joseph's first marriage, as there was some evidence for this. In the *Protoevangelium Jacobi* (Infancy Gospel of James) Joseph mentions his children when he protests at the request to take Mary as his wife: "'I have sons, I am an old man, but she is a girl: lest I become a laughing-stock to the children of Israel'" (Book of James 9:2).[1] This particular gospel was one of the best-known and most popular of the Apocryphal gospels. Because of the date of composition, *c.* AD 150, it cannot be Jesus' brother

James who was the author but, as we have seen, it was not unusual to give authority to a text by invoking the name of a well-known figure. While the details on Mary in this text closely match Luke's account, the issue of Mary's virginity is central here. In fact, a midwife is called upon to check that Mary's virginity has remained intact after the birth of Jesus.

From the earliest times, therefore, Mary's physical virginity becomes a central theme in the musings and writings of Christian thinkers, though neither St Paul nor St Mark, the earliest commentators, make any mention of a virgin birth. Moreover, the following passage suggests that there is no implication of perpetual virginity for Mary: 'When Joseph awoke from sleep, he did as the angel of the Lord commanded him; he took her as his wife, but had no marital relations with her until she had borne a son; and he named him Jesus' (Matthew 1.24–25). In other words, Joseph and Mary had a marital relationship *after* the birth of Jesus. This would tie in with convention and the fact of Jesus' siblings. Later, however, the Roman theologian Jerome decided that Jesus' siblings were actually his cousins, because Jerome wanted a virginal Joseph as husband for a virginal Mary.

When Jesus' birth is prophesied in Isaiah 7.14, the Hebrew word '*almah*', which means 'young woman' is used in relation to Mary. When 'young woman' was translated into Greek by the Christians, the word '*parthenos*' was used. This can mean girl or virgin. I was interested in the origin of the word 'virgin' and, having consulted various sources, I discovered that, in ancient myth, the word 'virgin' had no sexual connotations. It simply meant an unmarried young woman who was not beholden to a man. It was a word also used in conjunction with goddesses.[2] Christians introduced the idea of purity and chastity to the word, and thus began the link between Mary and virginity, rather than using the original description of Mary as simply a 'young woman', not yet married.

Bishop Augustine wrote that not only did Mary conceive without carnal desire, as she had been impregnated by the Holy Spirit, she was also rewarded by giving birth without pain.[3] We can only speculate about how such information came to light over 300 years after the event! However, you can see where this is going. The pains of childbirth are now being suggested as a punishment for the active participation in the conception of children. But by making this argument, Augustine is contradicting older Christian doctrine, as in Genesis, where the pains of childbirth are part of the list of punishments doled out by God to Adam and Eve for eating the apple from the Tree of Knowledge, not for having sex.

Bishop Ambrose of Milan was particularly influential in disseminating the idea of Mary's perpetual virginity. When he was writing, virginity was considered to be the supreme Christian virtue and he glorified it at every opportunity. For Ambrose, women carried the weakness of Eve in their bodies and consequently had to bear the yoke of inferiority, so it was inevitable that the physical aspect of Mary's part in the birth of Jesus would have to be manipulated to suit the attribution of sexual purity. Thus Ambrose rewrote the biography of Mary to make her 'fit' his ideal model of virginal womanhood. As a proponent of the supremacy of virginity, the 'miraculous' birth of Jesus, a notion that leaves Mary physically intact, so to speak, and unchanged, perfectly suited Ambrose's view.

The preoccupation with Mary's virginity has continued. As recently as 1987, John Paul II wrote in *The Mother of the Redeemer: Redemptoris Mater* (25 March 1987) that Mary 'preserved her virginity intact'.[4] Creating the idea of Mary as the perfect mother who is also a perpetual virgin had the advantage of removing all traces of sexuality from her representation.

In 1854 Pope Pius IX (1846–78) declared the dogma of the Immaculate Conception. The dogma of the Immaculate Conception actually refers to when Mary herself was conceived by her parents. This is because Mary, the mother of Jesus, could not be born with the stain of Original Sin as taught and promulgated by Augustine, who believed that it was transmitted from generation to generation by the sexual act. The dogma of the Immaculate Conception spares Mary from the stain of Original Sin, meaning that she is exempt from being born with sin. In this way, she is deemed worthy, by the men of the Church, of being the mother of Jesus. In contrast, the Holy Spirit did not seem to be particularly concerned about the technicalities. Mary was chosen to be the mother of Jesus. It was as simple and as extraordinary as that.

The new translation of the Roman Missal, introduced, or should I say, enforced, in 2011, implicitly negates the physicality of Jesus' birth. The phrase in the Nicene Creed, 'by the power of the Holy Spirit he was *born* of the Virgin Mary' now reads, 'and by the Holy Spirit was *incarnate* of the Virgin Mary' (my italics). 'Incarnate' means embodied in human form or made into flesh. It is a more abstract expression than 'born', which is an active word. In this way, woman's role is merely as an instrument of God's grand design for propagating the species. The words reinforce Ancient Greek biological beliefs about the womb acting merely as a passive receptacle for the male seed, thereby reasserting the priority of the male seed over the female womb.

It is difficult to understand today why it is not enough that Mary was chosen to be the mother of Jesus. We can only infer that the relentless focus on manipulating this natural phenomenon is because the topic comes under the umbrella of female sexuality, which is viewed in such negative terms in Church writings. Furthermore, it appears that the nineteenth-, twentieth- and twenty-first-century men of the Church continue to propagate fifth-century thinking. Mary was chosen to be Jesus' mother because the point of Jesus' mission was to identify with humanity, and thus he was born in the same way as all human beings are. Mary therefore does not, in my view, need any extra man-made attributes.

So the Church was able to create the perfect model woman in Our Lady, but what of an example of a female sinner who could be redeemed by a merciful Jesus? As mentioned earlier, the insertion of a story about an adulterous woman into John's gospel was the perfect example with which to depict a forgiving Messiah. But given that the most prominent woman in the gospels, Mary Magdalene, caused much debate as to her role and presence in the scriptures, she was the one eventually positioned as the most useful contrast to Our Lady.

Mary Magdalene's role in the story of the death and resurrection of Jesus is, to my mind, pretty clear and straightforward. She is the first witness of the resurrection in three of the four accounts, and Jesus asks her to spread the word to the disciples. Moreover, there is no question about her belief in what she has witnessed. Susan Haskins, in *Mary Magdalen: Myth and Metaphor*, notes that Jerome recognised the privilege bestowed on Mary Magdalene as being the first to see the risen Christ, as mentioned in a letter to his friend Principia.[5] However, his acknowledgement of Mary Magdalene's role in the gospels was completely overshadowed by the sheer volume of his writing on women's shortcomings. Jerome was a complex character. He had women friends who loved him and whom he appeared to love in return. Yet he could and did write extraordinarily emotional diatribes against women. Unfortunately, as Jerome served as secretary to Pope Damasus I and had undertaken the translation of the scriptures into Latin, his authoritarian-style letters were highly influential.

You will recall how the *Catechism* account subtly repositioned Mary Magdalene as first witness for the apostles. That stance has precedence. Here is Ambrose of Milan's account: 'Also, she is sent to those stronger than herself so that they preach the story of the resurrection to her, whose example will teach her to believe.'[6] That is quite a staggering reinterpretation of events. It seems that those who were not present at the events will tell Mary Magdalene, who *was* present, all about it! Furthermore, they will teach her, who already believes, to believe what she has seen. This fantasy account completely negates Mary Magdalene's status and aligns her with Ambrose's personal view of women as weak beings. In addition, it demonstrates how easily Mary Magdalene's mission to spread the word of Jesus' resurrection was reinterpreted to suit the particular male audience Ambrose had in mind for his writing. At the time, he was writing a commentary on Chapter 10 of Luke's gospel. This is significant as, first, this is the gospel that had the story of the 'sinful woman' who washed Jesus' feet with her tears; and second, it is the only account that mentions Jesus appearing to Simon Peter first after the resurrection.

Ambrose was the first to ask questions about Mary Magdalene's identity, especially as Mary of Bethany (Lazarus' sister) and Mary the mother of Jesus were also mentioned in the scriptures. This is despite the fact that Mary Magdalene's name is always given in full, clearly denoting her as a different person. Ambrose, like Jerome, and indeed Augustine, was curious as to the identity of the women in the Bible stories, and what their respective significance was in those stories. Put briefly, the Fathers of the Church confused, or more likely, merged Mary Magdalene with other women: Mary of Bethany, who is mentioned in Luke and John's gospels; the sinful woman in Luke's gospel; and, most especially, the woman who is condemned for adultery in John's gospel. In this way, Mary Magdalene became a sexual transgressor who had been redeemed by meeting Jesus.

Susan Haskins describes in more detail how the link to Mary Magdalene and sexual sin was made. In the longer ending of Mark's gospel, Mary Magdalene is described as the woman from whom Jesus 'had cast out seven demons' (Mark 16.9). Similarly, in Luke's gospel, she is: 'Mary, called Magdalene, from whom seven demons had gone out' (Luke 8.2). Mary Magdalene being cured of seven demons became associated with the seven deadly sins. Haskins, whose book

provides a detailed account of Mary Magdalene's 'transformation' from companion of Jesus to prostitute, explains:
'Fornication was a particularly female vice, it was deemed,
for woman was more carnal than man, as well as being more
imperfect from creation.'[7] Eventually, Pope Gregory I (c.
590–604), also known as Gregory the Great, in light of the
musings by Church writers about Mary Magdalene's identity and her role in the Bible, came to a decision about Mary
Magdalene that was to last for almost 1,400 years. He decided she was the sinful woman in Luke's gospel, and that the
seven devils ejected from her included the deadly sin of lust.
In that case, she was likely to be a woman who had committed adultery or debauchery of some kind. A woman forgiven
for her sexual sins by a benevolent Jesus was a much easier
character for the male hierarchy to deal with than a woman
in whom Jesus placed the important mission of witnessing
his death and resurrection. As a result, Mary Magdalene,
Haskins writes, 'became the redeemed whore and Christianity's model of repentance, a manageable, controllable
figure, and effective weapon and instrument of propaganda
against her own sex'.[8] In this way, Mary Magdalene, companion of Jesus, the first witness of the resurrection and the
messenger of the event of the resurrection, was reinvented.

Mary Magdalene was not relieved of her sinful imputa-
tion until 1969. Furthermore, it was not until 1978 that the
epithets previously attached to her name, 'penitent Mary' and
'great sinner', were removed from the Roman Breviary entry.[9]
However, the legend of Mary Magdalene as a prostitute who
is redeemed by meeting Jesus still lingers in popular culture,
such as in the musical, *Jesus Christ Superstar*, first staged in

1971. In addition, in Ireland, the Magdalene system, named after Mary Magdalene, was initially put in place for women who had become pregnant through prostitution. Laundry work was imposed as a form of punishment and penance for these women's sins. Later, the institutions housed any 'fallen' women – an example of the widespread judgement of one group of people by another. So, while Mary Magdalene's role as evangelist has been restored, her reputation has not. On the one hand, she now has a feast day in the liturgical calendar – 22 July – but, on the other, the Prayer of Pope Francis for the Jubilee of Mercy (2016) includes the words: 'Your loving gaze freed … the adulteress and Magdalene from seeking happiness only in created things.' The 'adulteress' and 'Magdalene' are linked by the assumption of sexual sin. This shows how deeply ingrained the belief about Mary Magdalene's reputation is, and how it persists, despite the wealth of research conducted about her.

Of course, if Mary Magdalene's role in the gospels was confronted, it would mean revising the idea of male-only apostles and disciples, as she has the requisite apostolic attributes. She is never considered in relation to the topic of priestly ordination, despite her presence with Jesus throughout his mission. As we have seen, she accompanies Jesus during his ministry, she witnesses his crucifixion, death and resurrection, and there is a tradition that she went to France to proclaim the good news. Thus, despite the 'rehabilitation' of Mary Magdalene's character in the twentieth century, residual antipathy to this woman, who does not appear to be attached to a specific man among Jesus' followers, remains.

Mary T. Malone, Susan Haskins and many others have argued convincingly in their work that Mary Magdalene was, at the very least, the leader of the group of women followers. Moreover, as Malone summarises in *The Elephant in the Church*:

> It is clear that Mary and her companions were the first witnesses of the Resurrection, the first proclaimers and preachers of the Christian message, and the ones who went to retrieve the men after the Resurrection, thus laying the foundation stones of Christianity. In other words, it is not difficult to call Mary of Magdala and her companions the true founders of the Christian Church.[10]

There is a text accredited to Mary Magdalene, the Gospel of Mary, which is considered to be one of the 'heretical' or Gnostic texts, and as a result, is not included in the Canon. Mary Magdalene is a central figure in this, as well as in many other texts, which were excluded during the third-century drive to impose conformity on scattered Christian communities by prioritising texts with the supposed authentic stamp of Peter and Paul. In the Gospel of Mary, Mary Magdalene steps up as a teacher in the aftermath of Jesus' violent death, when the apostles are upset and depressed. Needless to say, not all of the apostles, especially Peter, are happy about this, but Levi (or Matthew) defends her spiritual authority. His defence is interesting. He says to Peter: 'I see that you are contending against women like adversaries. But if the Saviour made her worthy, who are you to reject her? Surely the Saviour knows her very well. That is why he loved her more than us.'[11] The situation becomes quite testy, but there is no resolution or consensus reached among the apostles. It is unfortunate that Levi/Matthew's words have not been reflected upon. Moreover, the Church has down the ages continued to react to women as if they were adversaries.

The deliberate misrepresentation of Mary Magdalene provided the institutional Church with a model for sin, rehabilitation and redemption: in the Church's eyes a far more suitable role for a woman than that of witness to the resurrection. While Mary Magdalene's good character has quietly been restored, the Church has made no attempt to deal with the implications of her actual portrayal in the scriptures. This can only be because the Church is unwilling to acknowledge her presence in the context of Jesus' ministry. Her role as witness, a major feature of priestly succession, undermines the Church's position on the exclusion of women from the ministry. If Mary Magdalene is indeed an apostle, as St Paul similarly says of Junia, the nature of the priesthood would have to be reconsidered.

In any case, for our purposes here, Our Lady and Mary Magdalene serve as examples for the lengths to which representations of women in the Bible story have been manipulated to suit not only cultural but also sexist, and sometimes misogynistic, thinking. St Paul, as we shall now see, because of his authority as teacher, has also been mobilised to reverse women's roles in the Christian community, despite the proliferation of evidence in his letters that they worked alongside him.

ST PAUL AND WOMEN'S SILENCE

As St Paul's letters indicate, there was no distinction between the women and the men who worked alongside him. However, seeing women as equal in social and political terms was another matter. There is a passage attributed to St Paul, ordering women to be silent in church. In his first letter to the Corinthians, which was a response by him to a request for advice on local disputes that had arisen within the Corinthian congregation, there is the following pronouncement: 'Women should be silent in the churches. For they are not permitted to speak, but should be subordinate, as the law also says ... For it is shameful for a woman to speak in church' (1 Corinthians 14.34–36). This statement was adapted to bolster the argument for the abolition of leadership roles for women in the Church. But why would Paul make a pronouncement that contradicted the accounts throughout his letters of women working for the Lord?

The *HarperCollins Study Bible* explains that modern scholarship has established that this pronouncement on women's silence was a later addition to the letter and not attributable to Paul. The pronouncement may have been a reflection of Jewish law, as women were forbidden by Jewish law to speak in the temple. It may, therefore, have been an attempt by its author to reassert certain Jewish practices, as discussion about the inclusion of Gentiles and whether Gentiles should adopt Jewish practices continued for quite some time after Jesus. It also suggests that women *were* speaking at Christian gatherings. Additionally, Paul was generally even-handed in his treatment of the sexes. For example, in his directions on marriage, he said: 'For the wife does not have authority over her own body, but the husband does; likewise the husband does not have authority over his own body, but the wife does' (1 Corinthians 7.4). While a wife's subordination to her husband would have been a long-standing cultural norm in the ancient world, the concept of a husband's subordination to his wife would have seemed a radical idea. Moreover, Paul's letters clearly show that women played a central part in the communities he established.

The issue of women's silence also comes up in the first letter to Timothy, also formerly ascribed to Paul, where the unknown author makes the following pronouncement: 'Let a woman learn in silence with full submission. I permit no woman to teach or to have authority over a man; she is to keep silent' (1 Timothy 2.11–12). The author also includes a tirade against young widows (1 Timothy 5.11–16). Difficulties of translation make it impossible to discern whether widows were a specific group with a particular ministry at the time. In any case, the younger members or widows appeared to attract criticism from opponents of Christianity, which is perhaps the reason behind the author's diatribe. Moreover, given the context of composition, which is the concern with false teachers, and the tone of the letter, which implies a defensive stance, it is not conclusive that this order was meant to be permanent. Again, as with the insertion to Paul's letter to the Corinthians, the pronouncement contradicts Paul's inclusive attitude towards the women he greets in his letters.

The deliberate insertion of the pronouncement to one of Paul's letters by a later writer, and the former attribution of Timothy's letter to Paul, may have been a response to the threat of persecution. Suppressing radical elements of the new faith system, such as women leaders, preachers and teachers, would, for example, help to divert attention from the new religious movement. It is more likely, therefore, that such edicts were made in reaction to temporary circumstances. Whatever the reasons, by AD 200 it was an established view that had far-reaching consequences for women in the Church, as will be discussed later. Not only was it used down the ages to justify discrimination against women, but it was a perspective that was widely promulgated, while women's roles in the genuine Pauline letters as prominent figures in the new Christian movement were conveniently overlooked.

At the same time, it has to be said that Paul's attitude towards women is sometimes uneven. He is, after all, a man of his time. For example, he includes males and females in his call to leave behind distinctions and embrace unity in Galatians, but omits this in Corinthians (Galatians 3.28; 1 Corinthians 12.13). In his account of the final days of Jesus' ministry in his letter to the Corinthians, he does not specifically mention Mary Magdalene and the other women who were the first to witness the resurrected Jesus (1 Corinthians 15.5–8). Additionally, on the much-debated issue of women being veiled, he says 'any woman who prays or prophesies with her head unveiled disgraces her head' (1 Corinthians 11.5). Paul gets quite worked up about the subject, and the succeeding tirade about gender hierarchy, coupled with the difficulty of translation, means that there is much scholarly dispute about this section, although he appears to have been simply reflecting social conventions. It is likely that he did not want to draw attention to the nascent Church by having female prophets failing to reflect acceptable cultural behaviour, which dictated that women should be veiled in public. At the same time, however, Paul is acknowledging the existence of female prophets by talking about how a woman should be attired as she 'prays or prophesies'. That part of the passage has, of course, been overlooked. Again, this is an example of how, on the one hand, some interpretations are enforced with zeal – in this case, the wearing of head coverings, which women continued to do in church into the 1970s – while on the other, the fact of female prophets is ignored.

Not since the early Church movement have the voices of women been heard in Church affairs. As a matter of interest, from the fourth century onwards, women were forbidden to sing in church. In 1588 Pope Sixtus V went one step further by forbidding women to appear on stage at public theatres and opera houses in Rome and in the States of the Church. This ban remained in force throughout the seventeenth and eighteenth centuries. And even today, where can women speak? No woman's voice was heard during the discussions held at the Second Vatican Council, despite its radicalism. How can Church discussions therefore be inclusive of all God's people, when half of all God's people are women who are ordered to be silent?

Thus, for a religion that was considered radical for its time, Christianity underwent a remarkable change in its attitude towards women. The adoption of Jewish law, Roman organisational methods and St Paul's alleged pronouncements on women's silence in public created a view of women and their role in society that was accepted and eventually incorporated into the Christian mind-set. As little as fifty years after the time of Jesus, women's voices had been erased and, significantly, it appears that words positioning women as subservient to men were deliberately inserted into the scriptures in an attempt to restore the contemporary gender hierarchy that had been called into question by Paul's documentation of women in leadership roles. The eventual assembled Latin Bible consequently gave a theological explanation and justification for male dominance and female subservience in Roman Catholic culture.

The silencing of women does not, unfortunately, cover the full range of censure. Women's bodies were also targeted, particularly in the gradual enforcement of priestly celibacy. The drive to enforce priestly celibacy became inextricably linked with the evils of female sexuality, and as a result, women's sexuality became one of the primary concerns of the institutional Church. Thus, as we shall see, woman was positioned as the threat to man's pursuit of celibacy, rather than the decision to choose a life of celibacy being the concern of the man involved and nothing whatever to do with the women around him.

6

THE CELIBATE MAN VERSUS
THE CARNAL WOMAN

JESUS AND ST PAUL ON CELIBACY, SEXUALITY AND MARRIAGE

The most significant event in the downgrading of women in the Christian movement was the introduction and enforcement of priestly celibacy. Priestly celibacy is a discipline rather than a dogma. In other words, Jesus did not initiate the rule of priestly celibacy. Yet a Roman Catholic priest cannot marry: 'All the ordained ministers of the Latin Church ... are normally chosen from among men of faith who live a celibate life and who intend to remain *celibate* "for the sake of the kingdom of heaven"' (emphasis in original).[1] Interestingly, the rule does not apply these days to married former Anglican priests, dissatisfied with their Church's admission of women to the priesthood, who are allowed to train and practise as Roman Catholic priests. Considering the centrality of a celibate priesthood to the Roman Catholic faith, that is a considerable concession.

The discipline of priestly celibacy was a gradual and drawn-out process that proved difficult to enforce. This is because it is not, as St Paul explained in his first letter to the Corinthians, a divine instruction. Rather, celibacy was mooted and enforced by various popes for a myriad of reasons. However, the impact it had on the perception of women cannot be underestimated. This is because, to enforce celibacy, woman has to be positioned as the enemy – the temptress who would distract a man from his priestly mission.

Women, as the daughters of Eve and thereby linked to Eve's sin, which in the writings of Church Fathers morphed into sexual sin, were positioned as the temptation put in the path of the righteous man's road to perfection. In this way, the responsibility of the priest to uphold his vow is secondary. Moreover, to make celibacy attractive as a way of life, sexuality, especially female sexuality, had to be made repugnant. As a result, sex became an almost obsessive issue in Church thinking and writings. In *The Gospel According to Woman*, Karen Armstrong writes: 'Christianity is unique in having hated and outlawed sex and in making people feel guilty because they are sexual beings.'[2] While there were some level-headed views expressed, it was the sometimes bizarre and extraordinary ones that prevailed. What is striking, however, is how little Jesus has to say about sex, outside of the sin of fornication, considering the Church's excessive interest in this area.

As we know from the gospels, the first person Jesus called on to follow him was a married man known as Simon Peter, whose marital status would have been the norm for a Jewish man of that era. In other words, Jesus chose a married man as his follower. I shall reiterate this: the first apostle, Simon Peter, the rock – from whom, it is argued, the pope succeeds – was a married man. Celibacy was therefore not a demand made by Jesus of his apostles. You will note, however, that

Jesus deliberately choosing *married* men as apostles is not often emphasised.

In the absence of Jesus choosing celibate men as followers, a more complex argument was needed to support priestly celibacy, so a discussion that took place between Jesus and the apostles was used to support the ideal of a celibate priesthood. The discussion was about celibacy, marriage as a lifelong partnership, and divorce. According to Matthew's gospel, the Pharisees questioned Jesus about divorce on the basis of the famous teaching, 'what God has joined together, let no one separate' (Matthew 19.6). This idea of a lifetime union was a radical teaching at a time when men could divorce their wives for almost any reason. Moreover, society at the time was a polygamous one. Considering too that lifespans at the time were short, marital unions were not a major undertaking, in contrast to today's expectations. In light of Jesus' teaching, sexual freedom and the ability to offload one's wife at will would no longer be tenable, which is why the disciples were grumbling about it. As a result, they wondered if it would be better to remain unmarried, but Jesus replied: 'Not everyone can accept this teaching, but only those to whom it is given' (Matthew 19.11). In *Eunuchs for Heaven* Uta Ranke-Heinemann writes that the view prevailed in the Church that Jesus was talking about celibacy here, but she argues that Jesus was, in fact, talking about adultery.[3] It appears that Jesus presented the view that marital fidelity was the ideal to aspire to, but at the same time acknowledged that not everyone would be able to practise or accept this teaching. He also stated clearly that adultery is a permissible ground for divorce (Matthew 19.9).

The view that Jesus was talking about celibacy arose

because he went on to speak about eunuchs in the very next sentence, thereby leading interpreters to link erroneously teachings on adultery to celibacy. About celibates or eunuchs, Jesus said: 'For there are eunuchs who have been so from birth, and there are eunuchs who have been made eunuchs by others, and there are eunuchs who have made themselves eunuchs for the sake of the kingdom of heaven. Let anyone accept this who can' (Matthew 19.12). The final sentence spoken by Jesus here is important, as again he acknowledges that not everyone will be able to 'accept this', just as he similarly remarks about marital fidelity. So with regard to celibacy, while Jesus chose married men to follow him, he acknowledged that some followers would choose celibacy, 'for the sake of the kingdom of heaven' (Matthew 19.12). Thus his words on celibacy are a reflection of the different circumstances of his followers.

Jesus, it has to be said, was fairly dismissive of earthly ties such as family and spouses. He was a man on a mission, and because of its short span, he did not have the time to nurture familial relationships. In his case, therefore, celibacy, if indeed he was unmarried, was circumstantial.

St Paul, following the example of Jesus, did not enforce the rule of celibacy, though it was a way of life he chose for himself. Moreover, it is curious that Paul does not cite Jesus as the model for celibacy if it is supposed to be a higher calling. In his letter to the Corinthians, Paul wrote concerning celibacy: 'I wish that all were as I myself am. But each has a particular gift from God, one having one kind and another a different kind' (1 Corinthians 7.7). Consequently, Paul, while expressing his personal opinion that celibacy is best for those who want to dedicate their life to spreading God's word, does not make it a requirement. Rather, he advises: '[L]et each of you lead the life that the Lord has assigned, to which God called you' (1 Corinthians 7.17). Paul believed that Christ's return was imminent, 'the appointed time has grown short' (1 Corinthians 7.29) and, as a result, there was no time to be concerned about whether one was married or not. Spreading the good news was the primary consideration. Thus Paul, in a similar vein to Jesus, advised his followers to lead the life that had been assigned to them by the Lord. In addition, Paul reiterates that it is God or the Holy Spirit who is in charge of this calling, not other mortals.

St Paul also addresses questions raised about whether sexual intimacy is compatible with a life in Christ. Of married couples he says:

> Do not deprive one another except perhaps by agreement for a set time, to devote yourselves to prayer, and then come together again, so that Satan may not tempt you because of your lack of self-control. This I say by way of concession, not of command. (1 Corinthians 7.5)

Paul continuously stresses that everything he says is his own opinion, as he uses the expressions 'I say' or 'I and not the Lord' when expressing his views (1 Corinthians 7.1–40). Indeed, he specifically reminds the Corinthians that he is expressing his own opinion: 'I have no command of the Lord, but I give my opinion as one who by the Lord's mercy is trustworthy' (1 Corinthians 7.25).

While Paul clearly places a high value on celibacy, he

does not condemn marital sexuality. Rather, he suggests that marriage is better than attempting celibacy for the sake of it: 'it is better to marry than to be aflame with passion' (1 Corinthians 7.9). As a matter of interest, Paul makes no mention of the idea of sex being for the purposes of procreation alone. Moreover, Paul does not want people to be 'anxious', so while he promotes the idea that it is better not to be married if undertaking God's work, he says 'it is no sin' to marry. Furthermore, in the same letter, when speaking about the apostles, Paul asks: 'Do we not have the right to be accompanied by a believing wife, as do the other apostles and the brothers of the Lord and Cephas?' (1 Corinthians 9.5). The implication here is that various apostles and the brothers of Jesus and Cephas were accompanied by their wives. Clearly, neither Jesus nor Paul advocated deserting one's wife to do the Lord's work; nor, indeed, did they advocate foregoing marriage to undertake the Lord's work.

Staying with the theme of priestly celibacy, things become interesting after Paul. The letters to Timothy and Titus, formerly ascribed to Paul, throw further light on how the mission to spread the good news was perpetuated after Jesus. These three letters are concerned with leadership offices in the various churches and the threat to Christian communities posed by false teachers. While the addressees, Timothy and Titus, were Paul's co-workers (Acts 16–19; 1 Corinthians 4.17; Philippians 2.19–23; 2 Corinthians 8.23), scholars believe that the letters were actually written early in the second century by someone who appears to have known at least some of Paul's letters. The unknown author or authors used Paul's name to lend authority to the missives.

In the first letter to Timothy, the author gives instructions about behaviour, worship and the traits needed for leadership. He also lays down guidelines for bishops:

> Now a bishop must be above reproach, married only once, temperate, sensible, respectable, hospitable, an apt teacher, not a drunkard, not violent but gentle, not quarrelsome, and not a lover of money. He must manage his own household well, keeping his children submissive and respectful in every way – for if someone does not know how to manage his own household, how can he take care of God's church? (1 Timothy 3.2–5)

In other words, a married bishop was the norm. Furthermore, the experience of marriage and children is promoted here as a valuable life experience for a bishop's ministry. In fact, the author actually berates false teachers for forbidding marriage to office holders (1 Timothy 4.3).

Similarly, in the letter to Titus, the author addresses both elders or overseers and bishops. He requests that Titus appoint 'elders in every town, as I directed you: someone who is blameless, married only once' (Titus 1.5–6). Yet today's office holders must be celibate.

It is in the first letter to Timothy, you will remember, that the edict on women's silence and submission to their husbands is contained: 'I permit no woman to teach or to have authority over a man; she is to keep silent' (1 Timothy 2.12). The reason I include the quotation here is to show that, while the command about women having no right to teach was perpetuated and maintained, the benefits of marriage for bishops undertaking Church leadership was not. A bishop being 'married only once' is not understood as a permanent order, in contrast to the command for women to be silent, which is. If the piece about married clergy is no longer tenable, then why does the forbidding of women to teach still stand? This anomaly is explained by the Church using the argument that the edict about bishops is a metaphor. In this way, the bishop is positioned as a fatherly figure in relation to his priests and congregation, rather than to his wife and children, thereby keeping the priests and laity under his jurisdiction in good order and submissive to his rule. It seems they have thought of everything!

As we have seen from the words of Jesus, as well as in the letters of St Paul, there is no rule about the followers of Jesus, or indeed the apostles, having to be celibate. However, celibacy became a useful tool for the control of priests in terms of allegiance and also for the retention of property within the Church organisation. To make celibacy an attractive option, two things had to happen: it had to be promoted as a higher calling and superior Christian path, and at the same time, marriage or companionship with a woman had to be made less appealing to would-be priests. The first of these was easy to promulgate in theory, as the virtue of celibacy was a notion that had pre-dated Christianity. The second was more difficult, but given women's already poor image, not impossible. Besides, it seems to have been almost a natural instinct for many Fathers of the Church to downgrade women so as to reassure themselves of the merits of maintaining a celibate lifestyle. Eve was a perfect model for this exercise. By linking her to sexual sin, and in turn, yoking all women to Eve, all women could thus be deemed liable to tempt the virtuous churchman from his path of purity.

THE DRIVE FOR CELIBACY

One of the most damaging legacies from the story of Adam and Eve, from the female point of view, is the notion of woman as temptress. This derives from dubious interpretations of the story. The serpent tempts Eve to eat the apple from the tree of life. The serpent, I might add, 'was more crafty than any other wild animal that the Lord God had made' (Genesis 3.1). Having been persuaded, 'she took of its fruit and ate; and she also gave some to her husband, who was with her; and he ate' (Genesis 3.6). Adam does not, it should be pointed out, refuse to eat the fruit. Indeed, he makes no protest at all. God, of course, discovers what they have done:

> 'Have you eaten from the tree of which I commanded you not to eat?' The man said, 'The woman whom you gave to be with me, she gave me fruit from the tree, and I ate.' Then the Lord God said to the woman, 'What is this that you have done?' The woman said, 'The serpent tricked me, and I ate.' (Genesis 3.11–13)

Adam is quick to blame Eve, even though he too knew the consequences of eating the fruit. In contrast to the generations that followed, who emphasised the role of Eve in this story, God punishes *both* of them, because *both* of them gave in to temptation. Adam could have refused, as he knew they were forbidden to eat fruit from that particular tree. Eve is granted no 'mitigating circumstances' for being 'tricked' by the more cunning serpent rather than by a mere mortal as Adam was. Yet Adam's inability to withstand temptation as an equal sign of *his* moral weakness was not the view perpetuated through the ages.

In the first letter to Timothy, for example, the author subtly changes the account as follows: 'For Adam was formed first, then Eve; and Adam was not deceived, but the woman was deceived and became a transgressor' (1 Timothy 2.13–14). Not only is Adam completely exonerated here, but Eve, and Eve alone, becomes the sinner who is responsible for unleashing ills on the world. As this letter was originally attributed to St Paul, these words carried authority for centuries, and Eve thus became the model for all women, each one of whom was capable, unless they were strictly monitored, of tempting men from their virtuous paths.

The topic of whether Adam and Eve had had sex before their transgression and punishment was discussed and debated endlessly. Jerome's interpretation of the Adam and Eve story was that their sex life came after 'the Fall'. In a letter to his female friend Eustochium, he argued that as sexuality was a result of the Fall, it was sinful. He assumed that Eve had been a virgin before the Fall, and as a result, the Fall, in his thinking, became all about sex, which was now equated with sin. This association between the Fall and sexual sin had some historical basis: the *HarperCollins Study Bible* notes that Jewish legend had it that Eve was sexually seduced by Satan, the serpent, who appeared to her disguised as an angel. In any case, from Jerome's time the Fall became all about sexual sin and Eve morphed into the model for tempting a man into sex rather than tempting him to eat forbidden fruit. Jerome's legacy was therefore the promotion of sexual renunciation, as he despised marriage and sex to an extraordinary degree. Even married sex, he argued, was tainted with sin, a position he set out in letters to his female friends. Virginity, in his view, was the only answer to this quandary.

The next notable person of the Dark Ages to wade into the discussions about Eve, women, sexuality and sin was the bishop and theologian, Augustine of Hippo, who converted to Catholicism and was baptised by Ambrose in 387. Augustine cemented the process of demoting women to the status of temptress and therefore being in need of careful supervision, as he was obsessed with the difficulties of celibacy. His teachings, especially on the subjects of Adam and Eve and Original Sin, are believed to be sound Catholic doctrine. Indeed, as Ranke-Heinemann writes: 'The history of the Christian sexual ethic was shaped by him.'[4] Augustine decided, as had Jerome, that sex was tainted with the notion of sin, a belief that was to last for generations. It was a short step, therefore, to the declaration made by Pope Leo the Great (440–61) that all sexual desire is sinful in itself.

At this point, it might be interesting to know a little more about Augustine, whose story I am paraphrasing here from the works of Hans Küng, Mary T. Malone and Uta Ranke-Heinemann. If you are expecting a paragon of virtue, you are about to be surprised. Before his conversion, Augustine had lived with his mistress for thirteen years, with whom he had a son, Adeodatus. The couple had not conceived a second time because they adopted the rhythm method of contraception, which Augustine described in a work entitled *The Morality of the Manichaeans*. The Manichaeans, a sect to which Augustine had belonged before his conversion to Christianity, did not encourage procreation, as the spilling of seed was deemed dangerous to one's vitality. Thus Augustine's eventual transformation to a life of celibacy was not without precedence, as the Manichaean sect, in a similar vein to Christianity, also saw the celibate as being superior.

Augustine's family did not deem his mistress suitable for marriage and his mother persuaded him to banish her as she had chosen a more suitable bride for him. Augustine kept his eleven-year-old son with him but the boy died at the age of eighteen. As his designated bride was as yet too young for marriage, Augustine took a second mistress for a time. However, his regret and dismay, after his conversion, at his disloyalty to his mistress of thirteen years gradually transformed itself into contempt for sexual love. Additionally, he appears to have fought a constant battle with his body to bring it into line with his intellectual decision to embrace celibacy. The only way Augustine seemed to be able to sustain being a Christian celibate was by living in an all-male world. He shunned all women, even the women in his family. As soon as he was appointed bishop, he built a monastery and ordered all his priests to move into it. It does not take a psychologist to tell us that this is a person struggling with the suppression of his sexuality for the 'higher' purpose of celibacy. Needless to say, Augustine projected his personal difficulties with celibacy onto women. Many synods went on to condemn the presence of women unrelated to priests in clerical homes. And, following in Augustine's footsteps,

Pope Gregory the Great, Ranke-Heinemann writes, 'urged bishops not to share their homes even with their mothers or sisters'.[5]

The presence of the apostles' wives posed a dilemma for those who called for celibacy in the Church. The word for wife and woman in Greek is the same: *guné*. Jerome, the biblical theologian, when translating the New Testament into Latin, translated *guné* as woman, thereby enabling him to dispense with a spousal relationship between these women and the apostles. In that way, the apostles' wives became women helpers or serving women.[6] The Douay–Rheims translation of the Bible has, for example: 'Have we not power to carry about a woman, a sister, as well as the rest of the apostles, and the brethren of the Lord, and Cephas?' (1 Corinthians 9.5). Sister, in this sense, is understood to be a sister in faith or in Christ. Later, and building on this mistranslation, Gregory the Great initially advocated the principle that priests and bishops should love their wives as sisters, thereby paving the path for the elimination of women from the lives of those called to serve God so as to achieve the goal of a celibate priesthood.

As Catholic morality became sexual morality, which included the implicit denigration of women, the official Church now had the ammunition to promote and enforce celibacy. Yet celibacy proved to be a thorny issue from the earliest times, as well as a difficult rule to impose. In addition, enforcing the rule of a celibate clergy reinforced the growing split between the Eastern and Western Churches as, in contrast to the Eastern Church, synod after synod continued to reiterate the ban on married clergy in the Roman Church.

The situation waxed and waned from the fourth to the eleventh centuries, with little regularisation across the universal Church. Some bishops or archbishops imposed it on their priests, while others did not. Moreover, while the clergy were pledged to celibacy in parts of Europe, in practice it was an entirely different matter, as mistresses were often substituted for wives. Great Britain, for example, proved difficult to bring to heel, and in Ireland there were married bishops right up to the twelfth century.

There are some notable dates in the history of Church celibacy. In 325 the Emperor Constantine, as mentioned earlier, called the Council of Nicaea in response to the Arian heresy, which denied that Christ was truly God. The Council settled the question of Christ's divinity, but it also decided that no man could marry after ordination. In 385 Pope Siricius decreed that married men should not sleep with their wives after ordination. How the hierarchy planned to enforce this, I cannot imagine. In 1074 Gregory VII, an ardent champion of celibacy, who carried out widespread reform, insisted that all ordinands pledge themselves to celibacy. However, this was widely disobeyed. In 1123, at the First Lateran Council, clerical marriages were deemed invalid, and in 1139 matrimony was formally denied to ordinands. Thereafter, in the wake of the Second Lateran Council of 1139, Pope Innocent II (1130–43) ruled that no married man could be admitted to the priesthood.

The hierarchy, however, was not always aware of the marital status of ordinands, as at this time marriage itself had not yet been formalised. This meant that many priests still had wives. Many also had children, to whom their wealth was passed down. This was considered to some degree acceptable as long as those children went into the Church, as, in that case, the wealth remained under Church jurisdiction. However, the growing number of offspring of clerics who did not follow their fathers into religious life proved problematic, as they were inheriting Church property and money. A celibate clergy would eliminate this problem. Celibacy was also considered desirable in that it would enforce allegiance to the Church. The lack of it meant that loyalties were shared with family members, lovers and legitimate and illegitimate children. In other words, there was no control. It does seem, therefore, that the push for mandatory celibacy was driven by the desire for control.

At the Fourth Lateran Council of 1215, Pope Innocent III, the most powerful medieval pope, used his authority to win acceptance at the Council for the discipline of celibacy. Innocent was a deeply ironic name for this pope, considering his responsibility for a great deal of bloodshed during his almost twenty-year iron-fisted reign, a term I use deliberately as he believed in the absolute unquestioning authority of the papacy, which he enforced with zeal. He passed a staggering number of laws, composed a vast array of penances and pursued so-called heretics to an obsessive degree. He had a similar interest in reinforcing anti-Semitic views. From the time of this pope, who was in situ at the time of Francis of Assisi, the absolutist, monarchical-type pope came into being.

As noted earlier, the ideal of virginity as the highest attainment pre-dated Christianity. The thirteenth-century Doctor of the Church Thomas Aquinas was a particular enthusiast, as reading ancient philosophy was part of his education, and the Stoa, a school of philosophy that existed from *c.* 300 BC to AD 250 (from where we get the word 'stoic'), was particularly zealous about the renunciation of all pleasure, which appealed to him. Aquinas, building on these ideas, taught that the sexual act had a negative impact on mental ability. After all, how could such a serious sin *not* have dangerous repercussions? How else, too, could celibacy be positioned as worth pursuing? To make celibacy the ultimate path to Christ, the sexual arena had to be dotted with hidden traps that punished the non-celibate. As women were associated with carnality, it was a short step to position them as enemies of the celibate man.

Aquinas had many issues that troubled him with regard to women. Given the widespread acceptance of their inferiority at the time, he was at a loss as to why they were created. Here is a flavour of his thoughts on this dilemma:

> It can be argued that woman should not have formed part of the world as it was initially created. For Aristotle says that a female is a misbegotten male. But it would be wrong for something misbegotten and [hence] deficient to be part of the initial creation. Therefore woman should not have been a part of that world.[7]

Aquinas goes on to theorise that a woman is created only when there is a weakness in either the semen or in the body of the woman bearing a child. Still, he had to find some reason for woman's existence, considering that she is, whether he likes it or not, God's creation. Here is his eventual decision: 'But with regard to universal nature the female is not misbegotten but is intended by Nature for the work of generation.'[8] So there you have, in black and white, the decision made by the Church Father who is considered to be the most eminent in terms of Church teaching. Yet even in this capacity there were limitations, as at the time, you will recall, it was thought that women were merely the carriers of the man's seed and that their bodies played no active part in the creation of a child. As had been the belief of the Ancient Greeks, a woman was merely the vessel that held the child until its birth.[9]

What also becomes clear is that procreation, in terms of Church thinking, is concerned with man's seed above all other considerations. The ancients' view was that sexual activity drained one's energy because of the loss of semen. Thus the idea that the act should be conducted for procreation alone was a concept with a heritage that preceded Christianity. A man who restricted himself to sex for procreation alone was to be lauded for his control and maturity. For the celibate, seed preserved in the body, and not wasted or expended, ensured the enhancement of health and well-being. The prioritising of semen in theological thinking is one of the strands pertinent to the Church's opposition to homosexual sex, as the seed falls on barren ground, so to speak. Furthermore, the opposition to contraception is based on the idea that preventative measures interfere with the journey of the semen to the uterus. The concern with interfering with potential life did not arise until later. Nor did the physical demands of pregnancy and childbirth for women ever figure; it is all about the male seed.

Unfortunately, the Fathers of the Church were not content to concentrate their energies on their own choice of celibacy. In fact, their detailed writings on topics such as the attributes of semen, the sexual act, deviant sexual positions, bestiality, homosexuality, anal and oral sex, masturbation and how sex should be conducted so as to omit pleasure, while at the same time undertaking it for the purposes of procreation, would fill many libraries. The extent of the 'knowledge' of the Church Fathers is breathtaking. How they acquired such knowledge is another question entirely. The detail is excruciating and frequently nonsensical, as their views were often based on the limited biological knowledge available at the time. However, it has to be said that biological discoveries did not make much difference to long-held views in this regard, as it took an inordinate amount of time for the sexual act between married couples to be viewed as anything other than sinful and distasteful.

In the real world, Karen Armstrong posits that it is likely that sex was much less of a preoccupation for ordinary people, who at the time had short life spans, and whose concerns were far more focused on issues such as malnutrition, and on disease resulting from the lack of knowledge about hygiene, as well as the dangers of childbirth. Furthermore, sexual expectations in relation to personal fulfilment were low.[10] Yet, Ranke-Heinemann writes: 'Throughout the Middle Ages, immense importance was attached to questions such as when intercourse was permitted, when not, and for how long an offender had to do penance on bread and water if it occurred at the wrong time.'[11] The consequences of sin were a tangible fear among the laity, perpetuated by the reams of rules composed and preached about in this regard. As Ranke-Heinemann writes:

> Anyone who imagines that these prohibitions on intercourse during Lent, on feast days and before Communion were simply advisory, and that their infringement was not a grave sin rendering the married liable to severe penalties, is ignoring a millennium of very real tyranny and projecting the milder attitude of more modern times into the past.[12]

Current readers are probably wondering how the clergy would know what was going on in marital bedrooms but, as Ranke-Heinemann explains, the numerous rules and regulations about when intercourse was permissible were preached from the pulpits. In addition, the sacrament of confession had been introduced as a yearly undertaking by the Fourth Lateran Council in 1215. So texts that contained the questions that could be asked of penitents were composed. As the extent of sexual knowledge appears to have been broader in the clerical realm than among the laity, the realisation eventually dawned that the clergy were, in fact, giving people ideas about matters hitherto unknown to them. As a result, priests were advised to scale back on asking penitents leading questions.[13]

As celibacy was promulgated as a superior way of life, not much notice was taken of marriage by the Church. Ambrose and Jerome, for example, saw marriage as a poor second choice to celibacy, although Augustine was not quite as opposed to it as other Church Fathers, because he saw it as providing the building blocks of society. For a long time marital arrangements were, in the case of the individuals involved, Armstrong writes, 'their own business, not that of the Church'.[14] Moreover, she continues, 'Augustine and Aquinas may have said that marriage was a sacrament, but no ceremonial was devised to celebrate this sacrament.'[15] However, as priestly celibacy was gradually enforced, the realisation dawned that the regulation of marriages would ensure that ordinands were not married. As a result, the Church gradually took charge of the marriage ritual. Also, marriage served to help those who could not achieve the heights of celibacy. And if sexual activity had to be generative to be acceptable, marriage did at least contain the sexual act to interaction with one partner.

The formula of the seven sacraments that included marriage was drawn up in the twelfth century. But it was the ideology of the Protestant Reformation, and the ability of Puritans to capitalise on their skill at preaching, that gradually led to the development of the ideal of Holy Matrimony that survives to this day. This development was not a beneficial one for women, though, as Martin Luther (1483–1546), who coined the phrase 'in the home' later championed by the Victorians, had very negative views about sex and marriage. He believed that marriage was women's punishment for the sins of Eve, and thus positioned the husband in charge of the household and all who lived in it, just as Aquinas had similarly taught. With men in charge, alongside women's lack of access to education, the man of the house assumed an authority that infiltrated both culture and Church, and in addition, placed a new emphasis on the Christian family. This idea of hierarchy within the family unit suited the Catholic Church's mind-set, as it was a reflection of 'natural law', and was adopted into the Catholic Church's marriage ritual. The negative consequences of this were enduring, as the woman's identity became integrated with that of her husband, who was given the quasi-divine role of head of the household. As a result, men could, and did, treat their wives and children in any manner they chose without incurring censure. The sixteenth-century enforcement of the sacrament of matrimony was therefore a suitable means of ensuring that women were kept in line by their husbands.

If marriage was to be promoted and Christianised, however, women could no longer be considered purely as daughters of Eve, otherwise how could the superior man lower himself to marry such an imperfect creature? As we have seen, Aquinas, among others, deemed that women's civic and moral duty was to procreate and populate the world. However, procreation had to be regulated, as legitimate heirs were paramount to succession and inheritance. And women, if not kept in line, were thought to be liable to immoral and reckless behaviour, a view that pre-dated Christianity. Following the propagation of the Anglican and Puritan theologies of the seventeenth century, the role of woman as wife and mother was promoted as the ideal model of womanhood. In addition, controlling the sexuality of women by championing the virtuous mother whose only concern should be propagating the faith in her children was achieved by 'teaching' ordinary women to emulate Our Lady. In this way, women could be seen as weak and inferior, and in need of protection, rather than as temptresses.[16] Additionally, positioning women as weak beings in need of male guidance paralleled Church hierarchy in that the man ruled his wife and household just as God ruled the Church, and bishops their priests.

The Council of Trent (1545–63), which was established to counteract Protestantism, and assembled and reassembled over a period of almost twenty years, retained the rule of unmarried ordinands. It finalised the 'ritual' of marriage that took place before a priest and two witnesses, though the latter was not decreed as universal until 1908, with the promulgation of *Ne Temere*, which regulated Canon Law about marriage for Roman Catholics. The enforcement of this new marriage ritual ensured that priests or ordinands could no longer marry in secret or be accepted for the priesthood if they were already married. The Council went one step further by declaring celibacy and virginity as being superior to marriage. Only through celibacy could the path to perfection be achieved, it was declared, thereby excluding all but celibate, ordained men from the ranks.

However, the actuality of celibate priests continued to be difficult to enforce. Peter de Rosa gives a vivid account of the scale of decadence among the clergy in practice. For example, in Scotland, in the records of the Register of the Great Seal, which recorded the names and professions over a thirty-year period (1529–59) of men legitimising their 'bastard' children to facilitate inheritance, he notes: 'Every class of cleric was represented in the Register from cardinal to curate.'[17] Therefore, attempting to prioritise celibacy over marriage as the way to perfection resulted in widespread decadence.

For the Church, the dilemma arose frequently down the centuries: married priests or no priests; married priests or widespread fornication? To address this, the Council of

Trent introduced training for priests, which brought with it expected standards of behaviour, and gradually over the next fifty years or more, a uniformity of sorts was put in place. The rule of celibacy was therefore now in place. In reality, however, it is still a contentious issue. For example, in *Child Sexual Abuse and the Catholic Church*, Marie Keenan notes that recent studies in the USA suggest that up to 50 per cent of Roman Catholic clergy are sexually active at any one time.[18] The gap between the ideal and reality, therefore, is still wide.

Despite this, the eventual enforcement of the discipline of celibacy brought many advantages for the clergy. First, it created a new elite class, as the 'higher' calling of celibacy elevated the status of the priest over the people. This, in turn, implied an authority vested in the priest, which excluded the laity from the power structures of the Church, a situation that contrasted strongly with the early Church 'structure' consisting of the people, the leaders, and both lay and anointed preachers.

In the Christian mind-set, therefore, celibacy, sexuality and marriage are inextricably linked. Celibacy is the superior means of traversing the path to God, while marriage is suitable for those who are unable to attain that path. In addition, by ritualising marriage, sexuality is contained within marriage for the purposes of legitimate procreation and the sexual act must always be open to conception.[19] To summarise the Church's position on sexuality, then: every sexual thought, desire and action outside of marriage is a mortal sin. As Keenan explains, 'sexual misbehavior constitutes mortal sin in every instance. Hence, chastity is the norm that forms the basis of official Catholic thinking on sexuality.'[20] In other words, the denial of sexuality underpins edicts on sexuality. Thus the human norm in Church thinking is the celibate man.

Priestly celibacy was achieved at the expense of women's physical and moral representation. For the priest attempting celibacy, the women of his family could be lauded as models of the mother of Jesus, while those women to whom he was not related, and who were therefore a temptation, had the possibility of being redeemed, just as Mary Magdalene had been. The goal of celibacy, however, also bred a long-lasting antipathy to the idea of women as equal spiritual beings and reinforced the notion that women could not possibly be capable of maintaining any role of note in the Church organisation. Coupled with the objective of priestly celibacy, the vitriol and misogyny towards women expressed in the writings of certain Fathers of the Church, given the sheer volume of material, had to lead somewhere, and it did – to events that are rarely discussed.

THE FINAL ELIMINATION

The story of the elimination of the feminine from Christianity includes the persecution and execution of women over a period of almost 300 years. In 1484 Pope Innocent VIII (1484–92) began his reign by issuing an extraordinary papal bull, *Summis desiderantis affectibus*, which authorised two German inquisitors to act as they saw fit to combat the widespread belief in the morally weak; that is, witches. Two years later, *Malleus Maleficarum*, a handbook for witch-hunters, was composed and published by the inquisitors in question, Heinrich Kramer and Jacob Sprenger, both of whom were Dominicans. The handbook, which reproduced the text of Innocent VIII's papal bull, also contained extraordinary tirades against women's sexuality. Mary T. Malone writes: 'What the *Malleus* particularly planted in the imaginations of Christians in the sixteenth and seventeenth centuries was that witches were women, and these women were setting out to wreak havoc on male sexuality.'[21] There is no doubt that a central facet of this hysteria, in the context of maintaining the vow of celibacy, was the cleric's fear of giving in to sexual temptation, a fear that was projected onto hapless women. The handbook contained a good deal of superstitious nonsense, but was, unfortunately, highly influential, as the idea that the devil was prominent in the medieval world, especially in women given their association with Eve, was widely believed. At the time, the devil was the means of explaining the presence of evil in the world.

Witch-hunts had begun during the twelfth century, but while they were carried out sporadically during the following three centuries, the craze did not reach its peak until the sixteenth and seventeenth centuries. Scholars agree that attempting to explain the phenomenon is difficult, but an underlying feature was the obsession with enforcing what was considered to be 'the Truth' in the face of growing criticism of the institutional Church. As discussed earlier, attempts to impose orthodox or right-thinking beliefs and practices had begun as early as the second century. The Truth was taught by the bishops, who were the chief teachers and the successors of the apostles. Thus any sign of deviancy was viewed with deep antipathy by the Vatican, and the zeal to enforce orthodoxy was as a result of perceived threats to the Church's position. Malone recounts that movements arose again and again among the laity, who voiced concerns about the dominance of a hierarchical Church structure and questioned the power of the clergy in terms of believers having to go through them to access God, as well as pointing to the vast gap between Church practice and the example of Jesus in the scriptures.[22]

Rather than acknowledge wrongdoing (yes, it has form in this regard), the Church behaved like a despot. As Niccolò Machiavelli (1469–1527) advised in the sixteenth century manual on leadership and governance, *The Prince* (1532), as soon as a new Prince comes to power, he should strike down with force those who oppose him. Machiavelli, as it happens, was the chief adviser to Pope Leo X (1513–21), the fourth pope in a row, after Innocent VIII, to support witchhunts. This objective, of striking down opposition with force, was carried out with zeal, with the publication of Innocent VIII's document and the collusion of successive popes, each of which, you will remember, was not only Jesus Christ's stand-in on earth but also purported to be inspired by the Holy Spirit. The irony is that much of this campaign of violence took place during the period of the Renaissance and Reformation. The Reformation happened because Martin Luther had legitimate grounds for concern as the Church, at the time, was corrupt and greatly in need of reform. The reaction, then, was similar to that taken by the Vatican in the wake of contemporary clerical abuse scandals: the Church in Rome turned in on itself and concentrated on defending its position.

Although both men and women were accused of witchcraft and burned at the stake, it is women who, even today, are associated with the term 'witch'. It is impossible to ascertain how many women were targeted for reasons as diverse as an obvious love of nature or for their knowledge of medicinal herbs, but scholars have suggested that it may run into hundreds of thousands. Also included were scholars, gypsies, mystics and midwives. The latter were believed to be directly confronting God if attempting to ease the pain of childbirth, as labour pains were deemed to be God's punishment for Eve's sin. Any intervention by midwives was therefore a direct contravention of God's will. In short, women were watched, tried and executed for their supposed lack of conformity to the ways of the Catholic Church. Many scholars have attempted to understand why the witch-hunts occurred, but an explanation that casts sufficient light on such a prolonged campaign of brutality still eludes us. The proliferation of misogynistic and sexist writings that had gone before, which targeted women because of their nature and their sexuality, cannot fail to be a factor. It is hardly coincidental too that most of the victims were from the poorest classes.

The public nature of the brutal punishment of alleged deviants – torture, drowning and burning at the stake – ensured that the consequences of any perceived opposition to the Church would not be forgotten. Whatever the reasons, the outcome of this sustained brutality was the elimination of the feminine from the Church. It was now, as the men of the Church had wanted from as early as fifty years after Jesus, a woman-free zone. There is no question that 300 years of the targeting and execution of women lingered in the cultural psyche. It also reinforced the notion of the absence of women from the Christian story.

There is little doubt, in my view, that the imposition of celibacy was a direct factor in the persecution of women that began in the twelfth century and reached its hysterical pitch in the sixteenth and seventeenth centuries. Brutality, in the name of Christianity, has unfortunately frequently been part and parcel of the history of the religion. Additionally, while the Catholic Church did not initiate the denigration of women, it certainly perpetuated it by promulgating the role of Eve as temptress in the creation myth, and by focusing to an alarming degree on the unfounded sinful past of Mary Magdalene. We have seen how quickly attempts to exclude women from the Christian story began, and how women were sacrificed to achieve the goal of male celibacy within the priesthood. We shall now turn to look at how the Church maintained its position on the status of women in the Catholic Church in light of women's growing visibility in society, their access to education and their scholarly examination of Christian teachings.

7

DILEMMAS AND CONTRADICTIONS

THE MIGHT OF TRADITION

In the twentieth century, as women began to study and read the scriptures, the writings of Church Fathers, the work of theologians and historians, as well as papal writings, the anomalies between the scriptures and the early Christian movement, in comparison to the modern Church's stance on women, came to light. It became clear that Jesus had women among his followers. Moreover, Mary Magdalene was a close companion and she was given the privilege of being the first to witness his resurrection. Jesus also gave her the mission of speaking about his resurrection. In addition, the letters of St Paul clearly demonstrated that women led communities he had established and were key figures in sharing in his mission and work. In that case, the reasons stated by the Church for women's exclusion from ministry are not as absolute as we might have thought. Just to refresh our memories, these are:

(1) The example from Scripture of Christ choosing his apostles from among men.

(2) The constant practice of the Church, which has imitated Christ in only choosing men.

(3) The living teaching authority of the Church, which holds that the exclusion of women from the priesthood is in accordance with God's plan for his Church.

The Church needed a stronger pillar to shore up its stance, and in this case, Tradition, once again, provided that support.

Tradition, with its implied understanding of something long-established and authentic, is much used by the Roman Catholic Church as an argument for Truth. It is fundamental to the argument against the ordination of women. Its general meaning is understood as the transmission of long-held customs or beliefs from generation to generation. However, in relation to Christianity, the *Concise Oxford English Dictionary* defines Tradition as: 'doctrine not explicit in the Bible but held to derive from the oral teaching of Christ and the Apostles'.[1] The key phrases here are 'not explicit' and 'held to derive', as what one is left with is interpretation – and interpretation is, of course, subjective. This definition of the word in relation to Christianity therefore serves two functions: on the one hand, it invokes the words of Christ and the Apostles, while on the other, it implies an authoritative interpretation of those words.

In light of new historical, theological and feminist debate, the Church had to explain what it meant by Tradition. Pope John Paul II duly undertook this task, and the results were set down in the revised *Catechism*:

> Tradition is to be distinguished from the various theological, disciplinary, liturgical or devotional traditions, born in the local churches over time. These are the particular forms,

> adapted to different places and times, in which the great
> Tradition is expressed. In the light of Tradition, these
> traditions can be retained, modified or even abandoned
> under the guidance of the Church's Magisterium.[2]

In other words, there are two forms of tradition: one that is
fixed and one that can be changed. The various occurrences at
the beginning of the Christian movement are underpinned
by the 'great Tradition', which has a bigger picture in mind.
In that context, the fact of women sharing in ministry is
one of those temporary traditions, in much the same way
that it was decided in the second century that only certain
witnesses of the resurrection were to be considered authentic.
So, underpinning the evolving early Christian movement
was a greater Tradition, and in the greater Tradition women
should not have had the leadership roles they appeared to
hold in the temporary tradition.

Such teachings on the nature of Tradition(s) do not, of
course, explain logically or fully the continuance of some
beliefs, rituals and practices, and the dismissal of others, given
that the first few hundred years of the Christian movement
encompassed a variety of beliefs and practices. As we have
seen, rules such as celibacy took centuries to enforce, and
many practices – such as buying indulgences, eating fish on
Fridays, the obligatory Mass taking place only on Sundays
and so on – have quietly been discontinued or revised. The
Church's Magisterium is, as mentioned earlier, the teaching
authority of the Church and is guided by the Holy Spirit. We
can only surmise, therefore, that the Holy Spirit occasionally
guides the teaching authority of the Church to change its

mind about certain traditions. Infallible popes, however, do not have the same luxury. Obviously, that dilemma requires some explanation, and here it is. The Magisterium of the Church is defined in the *Catholic Dictionary* as:

> [the] Church's teaching authority, instituted by Christ and guided by the Holy Spirit, which seeks to safeguard and explain the truths of the faith. The Magisterium is exercised in two ways: *extraordinary*, when the Pope and ecumenical councils infallibly define a truth of faith or morals that is necessary for one's salvation and that has been constantly taught and held by the Church; *ordinary*, when the Church infallibly defines truths of the Faith: (1) taught universally and without dissent, (2) which must be taught or the Magisterium would be failing in its duty, (3) connected with a grave matter of faith or morals, and (4) which is taught authoritatively. Not everything taught by the Magisterium is done so infallibly; however, the exercise of the Magisterium is faithful to Christ and what He taught.

In other words, equal weight is given to the pope's 'apostolic authority', the Magisterium or teaching authority of the Church and the scriptures. The Magisterium is therefore at liberty to make decisions about whatever it likes, provided it can be seen to be justified by citing scriptural authority, even if that authority is based on a flawed interpretation of the scriptures. However, there is some room for anomaly, as not all Magisterium teaching is done 'infallibly'. In addition, as the group is, we are told, guided by the Holy Spirit, no argument against the Magisterium can be sustained. As one cannot argue with the Holy Spirit, this teaching of the sanctity of 'the great Tradition', it has to be said, is a masterstroke.

However, as Tradition in the context above still contains much ambiguity, tradition and scripture needed to be linked more effectively, and here is how this interconnection is explained:

> "Sacred Tradition and Sacred Scripture, then, are bound closely together, and communicate one with the other. For both of them, flowing out from the same divine well-spring, come together in some fashion to form one thing, and move towards the same goal." ... "*Sacred Scripture* is the speech of God as it is put down in writing under the breath of the Holy Spirit." "And [Holy] *Tradition* transmits in its entirety the Word of God which has been entrusted to the apostles by Christ the Lord and the Holy Spirit." ... As a result the Church, to whom the transmission and interpretation of Revelation is entrusted, "does not derive her certainty about all revealed truths from the holy Scriptures alone. Both Scripture and Tradition must be accepted and honoured with equal sentiments of devotion and reverence."[3]

If your head is swimming, that is the general idea. Such an argument requires protracted, wordy explanations and the theoretical teasing out of ideas. However, there are a few things of note here. First, the use of 'in some fashion' to describe how the two, Tradition and Scripture, come together. In other words, there is no definite way to link the two. Second, the 'Word of God' was entrusted solely to the apostles (even though the gospels cannot have been written by the apostles). My understanding here is that while the scriptures report what Jesus said and what he said about God, these reported words, coupled with the *interpretation* of what was said, are considered to be the 'Word of God'. The term 'Word of God' also includes what those who interpret his words think was intended for the future. And included in this 'intention' is the idea that the exclusion of women from Catholic Church ministry is what God intended, and is, therefore, 'in accordance with God's plan for his Church'. Finally, while the Church 'does not derive her certainty about all revealed truths' from the gospels, by employing the notion of Tradition, and by giving it the same weight as the sacred scriptures, the argument is given authority and credence. The final sentence is a veiled order: if the scriptures are not clear, Tradition must suffice and, furthermore, it must be accepted as being equal to the scriptures. In other words, interpretation of the scriptures, when promulgated by the pope and/or the Magisterium, must be accepted without question. The views of the people of the Church – theologians, bishops and clergy – therefore count for very little.

Despite the veiled order to accept all Magisterium and papal teachings without question, many have difficulty in doing so. However, when 'tradition' is questioned and found wanting, there is one more trump card that can be played, and that is the doctrine of papal infallibility. Any examination of Church history clearly demonstrates that popes in the past were fallible long before they were deemed infallible, as bad decisions were made by various popes on the basis of misinterpretations of Church teachings, as well as for altruistic reasons. There is some dispute over when papal supremacy and infallibility was declared – either in 1302, when Boniface VIII (1294–1303) made it a Church doctrine for the laity to obey the pope in all matters; or during the First Vatican Council presided over by Pius IX, when the dogma of infallibility was defined.

The First Vatican Council, which opened in 1869 and was never formally closed, defined the special gift or charism of papal infallibility as the inability to make a mistake when teaching the truth on doctrinal issues. The outcome of various decrees at this council was described by Peter de Rosa as follows: 'The distinct impression was given that, far from the pope getting his faith from the church, the church gets its faith from the pope.'⁴ The idea of any human being, whatever the human role given to them in Church or society, being infallible is breathtakingly arrogant. This is especially so given that numerous popes in the history of the Church were, without question, not only fallible, but also immoral, cruel and depraved. Popes are, after all, human beings and are subject, like all of us, to ordinary human frailties.

The result of this relatively recent edict, however, is complex. For example, when the pope is said to speak *ex cathedra*, as the *Catholic Dictionary* explains, 'so as to bind the universal Church', he has to be cognizant of the utterance of every preceding pope. This places the pope in an impossible situation, as he has to be careful not to contradict or put into question previous papal edicts. What this means in practice is that popes are never wrong when they speak as head of the Church. As a result, the pope cannot, for example, formally declare that previous edicts and doctrines supporting acts such as the persecution of Jews, inaction on slavery, the

Inquisition trials, the slaughter of heretics (anyone whose outlook the Roman Church disliked or denounced) during the Crusades, the witch-hunts, and so on, were wrong. Instead, former traditions, such as unbaptised babies remaining in Limbo for eternity, are quietly re-evaluated and reworded in ambiguous language that carefully avoids outright condemnation of former interpretations.

As a result, the Church has fallen into a trap of its own making in that it is extremely difficult to apply normal cultural, developmental and evolutional thinking to the practices and edicts of the institutional Church. Consequently, in contrast to the early Christian movement and the early Church, where faith and morals were discussed, debated and interpreted from a myriad of texts, in the contemporary institution faith and morals are decided on by the Magisterium and the pope. Contradiction or debate is not encouraged as it may interfere with the ideal of 'bind[ing] the universal Church'. In this context, therefore, it can be argued that the dogma of papal infallibility was a useful one to adopt, as it dispenses with any obligation to discuss matters of faith and morals in depth with either the ordinary clergy or the laity.

The deployment of the 'great Tradition' theory means that the argument about the ordination of women cannot be resolved as long as this mind-set prevails. Equally, women cannot be expected to accept such an ad hoc set of bizarre reasons 'proving' that the Holy Spirit does not call on them to serve. That is why women and the Church are in deadlock. Women are not on a level playing field. Invoking the authority of the Holy Spirit is unjust, as in this context, the Holy Spirit, rather than the Church itself, which is of course the case, is positioned as being sexist. If that is the situation, it is a short step to decide that the Holy Spirit is also racist or homophobic, as the language of exclusion for any category of humanity is the same. In actual terms, the Church's view understands that the Holy Spirit is indifferent to the talents of women – that is, half of humankind – and does not deem them suitable to serve God.

'ALL OF YOU ARE ONE'

> There is no longer Jew or Greek, there is no longer slave or free, there is no longer male and female; for all of you are one in Christ Jesus. (Galatians 3.28)

Jesus called for a new community, with a new sense of identity based on being a follower of Christ. The barrier of difference or exclusion – race, status or gender – 'is no longer', Paul wrote. Yet, despite the fact of Jesus' Jewishness, as well as Paul's mission to unite Jews and Gentiles in the new Christian movement, the Church supported a long history of anti-Semitism. In the second-century letter to Titus, the context is concern about false teachers. It is Jewish ones in particular that incur the author's wrath: 'They are detestable, disobedient, unfit for any good work' (Titus 1.16). The anti-Jewish stance, based on the diatribe about false Jewish teachers in the letter, as well as the role of the Jews in the death of Jesus, was held by the Roman Catholic Church for thousands of years. It was not until 1960 (though the matter was raised in the 1920s) that the negative adjectives (faithless, perfidious) formerly used to describe Jews were removed from the Good Friday prayer for the Jewish people. That is quite a turnaround.

In addition, because Jesus only spoke against slavery but did not actually abolish it, the Church supported slavery long after it was reasonable to do so. In the letter to Titus, slaves were exhorted to be completely submissive to their masters, just as women were required to be submissive to their husbands. Slaves frequented the pages of the Old Testament and the papacy argued that slavery was the will of God, which is the interpretation of God's will as revealed in the scriptures. Thus 'natural and divine law', according to the Church, understood that it was acceptable to buy and sell human beings. At a time when slavery had been abolished in most civilised countries, a document signed by Pope Pius IX in 1866 stated: 'It is not contrary to the natural and divine law for a slave to be sold, bought, exchanged or given.'[5] In other words, rather than leading the way, the Church showed great reluctance to accept that slavery was wrong. In fact, the Catholic Church supported slavery for nineteen centuries, a 'tradition' that it eventually conceded was unacceptable. 'Divine' support for slavery was not withdrawn until the Second Vatican Council.

As a result of Jesus' mission, 'I have come not to abolish but to fulfil' (Matthew 5.17), many of his words and actions are subject to interpretation. This is why the Church has overturned stances previously held with regard to its misinterpretation of the role of Jews in the story of Christianity, as well as the rights of owners to have slaves. Why, then, cannot the same attention be given to the role of women in the Church – 'there is no longer male and female'? Contrary to what the Church states, cultural and evolutionary contexts are relevant, as how else can the abolition of slavery and the dropping of the anti-Jewish stance be explained? Yet the Church decrees that the cultural context argument is not relevant in relation to women. This is another example of the Church's ability to hold a contradictory position on a particular issue. It can be argued that the antipathy towards women that resulted in the 300-year campaign of brutality towards them cannot but be an underlying factor in this context. The distrust, fear and misogyny that fed such brutality is so deeply rooted in the psyche of the institutional Church that it fails to recognise its significance.

To sum up the current situation, then: the abolition of expressions of anti-Semitism means that the distinction between Jew and Greek is dispensed with; the anti-slavery position abolishes the distinction between slave and free; yet, the distinction between male and female is retained.

As we have seen, the Church teaches that women cannot 'follow' Jesus in any official capacity, though Jesus himself does not appear to have shared that view. At no stage did he dismiss women from his group. Instead, he showed by both his example and his words that all humankind is equal in the sight of God. During his ministry, Jesus spoke to women, healed them and forgave them, just as he did with the men he encountered. Moreover, Jesus spoke up for women at every opportunity. Considering the position of women in society at the time, Jesus' behaviour towards them was radical. The disciples certainly thought so, as they often admonished him for exactly that.

It appears that St Paul attempted to emulate Jesus' example, and his is the earliest account of the burgeoning Christian movement that we have. His letters relate the facts of women colleagues and women in leadership roles in the early Christian movement. He too asked his followers to embrace a new way of life and a new type of community based on shared values rather than on race, gender or status. Unfortunately, the words inserted into Paul's letter about women's silence by a later author, clearly with a personal agenda, were attributed to Paul as authoritative teaching and have been used ever since to position women as being secondary to men. Furthermore, as later letters in the New Testament demonstrate, including those mistakenly attributed to Paul, the inclusion of women as co-workers in the community was not practised everywhere. Thus the difficulty of accepting women as equals can be found from very early on in Christian writings. Contemporary cultural practices, therefore, in contrast to the actions of Jesus, proved a strong force to overcome, and many Christian men could not accept or adopt Jesus' views on the value of all human beings.

So how was this new community supposed to work without the usual means of unity? St Paul, following in the footsteps of Jesus, preached the message of a new community with baptism and faith as the common factors: 'But now that faith has come, we are no longer subject to a disciplinarian, for in Christ Jesus you are all children of God through faith. As many of you as were baptized into Christ have clothed yourselves with Christ' (Galatians 3.25–27). Through baptism, therefore, all would be a part of this new movement and all would receive the Holy Spirit. The importance of this ritual is supported by the fact that the baptism of Jesus by John the Baptist is recorded in all the gospels (Matthew 3.13–17; Mark 1.9–11; Luke 3.21–22; John 1.29–34). In all accounts, it is written that the 'Holy Spirit descended upon him'. The gospels indicate that baptism is the means of receiving the Holy Spirit. It is that which transcends social and cultural differences (and gender, it has to be said), to make us one 'in union with Christ Jesus'. In other words, baptism is the criteria for membership of the Christian movement. That is the one common factor among Christians – not race, status or gender.

The Church teaches the following in relation to the sacrament of baptism: 'From the baptismal fonts is born the one People of God of the New Covenant, which transcends all the natural or human limits of nations, cultures, races and sexes: "For by one Spirit we were all baptized into one body".'[6] This seems to suggest that the Church agrees that baptism is the rite for becoming a Christian. It follows, therefore, that if all men and women are admitted to the 'one People of God' by baptism, and all are 'made to drink of one Spirit', that both men and women share in the divine in the same way. So far, so good. The teaching continues: 'The three sacraments of Baptism, Confirmation and Holy Orders confer, in addition to grace, a sacramental *character* or 'seal' by which the Christian shares in Christ's priesthood and is made a member of the Church according to different states and functions.'[7] Thus baptism is the sacrament that cleanses the baptised person of Original Sin, confers membership of the Church on the recipient and is a means of receiving the gifts of the Holy Spirit. In a similar vein, confirmation invokes the gift of the Holy Spirit on the baptised person. All three sacraments are a means of sharing in Christ's priesthood. Again, so far, so good.

However, there is now a short but forceful proviso at the end of the quotation: 'according to different states and functions'. Church membership therefore has categories. In this way, the sacrament of Holy Orders can be restricted to men, as only men can 'function' as priests. Ordination, the *Catholic Dictionary* explains, is the 'act of consecrating or setting apart of men to be the sacred ministers for the worship of God and for the sanctification of all people'. Here, as in the other two sacraments, the recipient receives spiritual power and grace. The question is, why are gender distinctions introduced into the sacrament of ordination? Why is it that only men are 'set apart' for this particular sacrament if all 'share in Christ's priesthood' through the sacraments of baptism and confirmation? In all other cases, the sacrament stands by itself, so to speak, and whom it is bestowed upon is not relevant.

The world we live in today has changed significantly since the 1960s, and it will continue to do so. Former 'categories' such as race, ethnicity, sexuality and gender are gradually, though painfully slowly, being eroded as barriers of distinction. As this exploration has noted repeatedly, Jesus sought to erase such distinctions. In contrast to his example, as Karen Armstrong writes: 'Throughout Christian history we have seen that it is separation which has been the dominant motif, not togetherness.'[8]

CONFLICT, CENSURE AND POPE FRANCIS

Despite the attempts to keep women out of the Vatican, the faithful continue to discuss the issue. However, the scale of the antipathy to the idea of women as ordained persons can be gleaned from the reaction by Rome towards anyone expressing the opinion that the matter should be discussed properly. As recounted earlier, the sin of attempting to ordain a woman is now under the jurisdiction of the same body that investigates child abuse cases. This includes the censuring of any religious personnel expressing the opinion that women can and should be ordained if they feel called to do so. The Congregation for the Doctrine of the Faith has been very active in this regard. Indeed, it has been amazingly swift in addressing and investigating dissidence with regard to female ordination, which, in light of their previous reluctance to deal with child abuse investigations, is striking. Moreover, the actions of the Church suggest a determination to enforce uniformity among the clergy and religious personnel as well as among the laity.

Let us look at a few examples. We shall begin with Fr Tony Flannery, an Irish priest born in 1947 who wrote for the Redemptorist publication, *Reality*, among others, until 2012. In that year, he was removed from his ministry, forbidden to publish any further articles and ordered not to speak to the media. An article Fr Flannery had written in 2010 for *Reality* proved objectionable to the Vatican. The bone of contention was Fr Flannery's opinion, as described by Douglas Dalby in *The New York Times*, that he no longer believed that 'the priesthood as we currently have it in the church originated with Jesus', or that Jesus designated 'a special group of his followers as priests'. Fr Flannery had written, 'It is more likely that some time after Jesus, a select and privileged group within the community who had abrogated power and authority to themselves, interpreted the occasion of the Last Supper in a manner that suited their own agenda.'[9] As we have seen from our explorations, Fr Flannery's remarks are not without foundation.

As well as being ordered to recant his remarks, the Vatican wanted Fr Flannery to write, sign and publish his affirmation that Christ instituted the Church with a permanent hierarchical structure, and that bishops are divinely established successors to the apostles. This is, of course, a perfectly logical request, as the sacramental nature of the priesthood is a matter of fundamental Catholic teaching. To write such an affirmation, however, 'goes against everything I believe in,' Fr Flannery remarked. As the order to dismiss him was conveyed to his religious superior, Fr Flannery had no means of either personally explaining his position or negotiating with any Vatican official. As a result, he remains dismissed as well as 'dissident'. It should be noted that Fr Flannery has been expressing his views about women and the priesthood, as well as questioning Church teachings on homosexuality and contraception, for decades, but the move by Benedict XVI to put an end to the matter in 2010 was vigorous. It appears that questioning the origins of the male-only priesthood was a step too far. Fr Flannery has written an account of this affair, entitled *A Question of Conscience* (2013).

In a similar vein, Fr Roy Bourgeois, a former Maryknoll missionary priest in the USA, who was excommunicated at the age of seventy in 2008 and laicised in January 2013, had expressed the view that nobody can say who God can and cannot call to the priesthood, and furthermore, that placing a barrier of anatomy on God's ability to call a person to the priesthood places a limit on God's power.[10] Fr Bourgeois was excommunicated for presiding at an ordination ceremony for a woman in the United States. He believes that the Vatican should open up the question of women's ordination for discussion and explains that for him it was a matter of conscience and that he had arrived at this conclusion over a long period of time and after conversations with many women who spoke of their calling to a priestly vocation.

Let us put some perspective on these incidents. In the same time-frame as the eager and vigorous clean-up on dissidence, the Vatican was extremely reluctant to impose laicisation on priests charged with criminal behaviour. Mick Peelo, the presenter of the RTÉ One programme *Would You Believe* transmitted on 17 January 2011, related that in the 1990s, when bishops headed by Cardinal Connell pleaded with Rome to address the issue of defrocking priests who had abused children, they had a difficult time convincing the Vatican. Moreover, the Vatican tried to block the Irish bishops from enforcing their collective decision to report all serious allegations to the gardaí. As Bishop Michael Smith related in the programme, the Vatican saw it as a moral issue rather than a crime, thereby placing the priest at the centre of the discussion rather than the victim. This view stems from the duty of a bishop always to support his priest in what effectively mirrors a father–son relationship. The Irish bishops repeatedly attempted to convince Rome that these men had committed crimes that had had a widespread effect on the children and the children's families, as well as on wider society.

In 2001, after sustained pressure from English-speaking bishops, Cardinal Ratzinger, who would become Pope in

2005, began to listen, but he faced strong opposition from two influential and powerful men: Cardinal Hoyos (President of the Pontifical Commission 'Ecclesia Dei') and Cardinal Bertone (Secretary of the Congregation for the Doctrine of the Faith). In 2004, however, Ratzinger broke ranks to investigate the allegations of corruption and abuse made against the founder of the Legion of Christ, Fr Marcial Maciel Degollado. However, he did not follow this through, and Maciel Degollado was not defrocked. Instead, he was sentenced to a life of penance; he died in 2008. Currently, while the Congregation for the Doctrine of the Faith has undertaken to accelerate their investigations of erring priests, they are not obliged to hand them over to the civil courts. In addition, Canon Law guidelines, which require that justice be restored to victims, have not been implemented. It appears that suppressing discussions about women being ordained is of far more concern to the Vatican than dealing with criminal priests. It is important to acknowledge at this point the extent to which women are *not* wanted in Catholic Church ministry.

In another move, as surprising as the elevation of the crime of ordaining women and in the midst of widespread recession, the Catholic Church introduced the hugely expensive undertaking of revising the Roman Missal to, it was stated, a more authentic and traditional translation of the Latin Bible. The Latin Bible is closely identified with the later institution of the Church, particularly the gradual collection of laws that culminated in Canon Law. It is difficult to see the introduction of the revised translation of the Roman Missal, which was imposed in November

2011, rather than being discussed, as anything other than a reminder to all Catholics of the power that the Roman hierarchy can exercise at will. It should be noted that the revised translation was imposed on priests as well as on the laity. Indeed, the Irish bishops refused to address the concerns about the new translation raised by the Association of Catholic Priests (ACP), a refusal that speaks volumes about hierarchical perceptions of power. The revised text reinstates the old, male-centred perspective, as the Latin Church, unlike its earlier formation model, eschewed any space for either the female voice or for female experience. The move to what the Church deems to be a truer adherence to the original Latin translation of Church texts is therefore a regression to the earlier male-orientated perspective of the Latin Church. It was also, in my view, an action similar to that taken in relation to the ordination of women. Rather than confront and discuss the question, the Church chose a defensive action to reinforce its authority and close off any discussion about revised interpretations of the scriptures.

The prevailing ethos of Catholicism communicated by Rome up to the retirement of Pope Benedict XVI appeared to be about reiterating the hallmarks of the 'proper' Catholic. We have seen how, in the past, the Church treated 'misfits': they were tortured, burned at the stake and, in our own time, abused, locked up in institutions, censured and excommunicated. These are hardly the actions of a Church founded on the maxim to love one another. Rather, such actions are tangible indications of the imposition of made-up rules and the consequent misuse of power. As a result, the Catholic Church has become an alien entity associated with sexism, cruelty, sexual and physical abuse, and the misuse of power. For the thousands of nuns, brothers, priests, bishops and lay people who work actively to alleviate the suffering of others all over the world, every single day, this is a difficult situation. There are numerous accounts of religious personnel engaged in serving others who do so without categorising the recipients of that help. Current perceptions of the Catholic Church, therefore, mean that this work is overlooked and under-appreciated in contemporary public discourse.

The appointment of Pope Francis has brought a different tone to the papacy. In *Evangelii Gaudium*, the Pope wrote:

> The Church is called to be the house of the Father, with doors always wide open. One concrete sign of such openness is that our church doors should always be open, so that if someone, moved by the Spirit, comes there looking for God, he or she will not find a closed door. There are other doors that should not be closed either. Everyone can share in some way in the life of the Church; everyone can be part of the community, nor should the doors of the sacraments be closed for simply any reason.[11]

Pope Francis' apostolic exhortation uses the metaphor of 'open doors' throughout. However, you will remember that at his impromptu press conference held aboard the papal plane in July 2013, as Patsy McGarry reported, Pope Francis said: 'on the ordination of women ... *that door is closed*' (my emphasis).[12] Not only are 'the doors of the sacraments', in this case, ordination, closed, they are 'closed for simply any reason', which is women's gender.

Pope Francis is attempting to change some aspects of the institution. For example, he is anxious to change the imperial image of the papacy, which is one of the reasons he does not live in the papal apartments. He has chosen eight cardinals from all over the world to help him with decision-making. He wants freedom of speech to be a matter of course at Synods, and indeed, the convening of the Extraordinary Synods on the Family in October 2014 and October 2015 was a radical step in Church history. The purpose of the 2014 Synod was to proclaim the gospel in the context of the pastoral challenges facing families today. In preparation for the Synod, the Vatican asked national bishops' conferences around the world to seek the opinions of Catholics on a number of Church teachings, including contraception, same-sex marriage and divorce. The 2015 Synod was a continuation on the theme of the family. And, it should be noted, the subject of allowing for female deacons was raised by Canadian Archbishop Paul-André Durocher of Gatineau, Quebec, at the 2015 Synod. However, while the opinions submitted by Catholics were collated and considered up to a point, the Synod members are all celibate males. Moreover, while women can speak at the Synods, they do not have voting rights. It is therefore difficult to see how the information received can be useful if it is streamed through such a narrow perspective.

The Pope has said that women should be involved in the institutional Church. On numerous occasions he has said that the Church needs 'to reflect in a more profound way on the dignity of Woman'. As part of the exercise of reflecting on the 'dignity of women', Mary Magdalene's reputation has been revised to reflect her actual portrayal in the Bible. In a decree issued in June 2016, the memorial day of St Mary Magdalene was elevated to become a Feast Day. This was done in acknowledgement of her role as proclaimer of the message of Easter. Moreover, the decree formalising the decision was entitled 'Apostle of the Apostles', a phrase, you will be surprised to learn, also used by Thomas Aquinas to describe Mary Magdalene. The Congregation for Divine worship and the Discipline of the Sacraments acknowledged that Mary Magdalene had been mis-identified in the past, 'with the woman who anointed Christ's feet with perfume in the house of Simon the Pharisee, and the sister of Lazarus and Martha'.[13] It is also acknowledged that she accompanied Jesus as one of his disciples and was the first witness. However, there is a proviso. For some reason I cannot fathom, the men of the Church appear incapable of presenting any woman in her own right. Thus, in this document, Mary Magdalene is now depicted as a contrast to Eve because she can no longer, given her status as holy woman, be a contrast to Our Lady. The document states: 'The first spread death where there was life; the second announced life from a sepulchre, the place of death.'[14] I can only surmise that in this way, Mary Magdalene now serves as an instrument for reversing or atoning for Eve's (all women's) sin. In my view, that supposition is confirmed in the last line of the document: 'she who is an example and model for all women in the Church'. The fact that the men of the Church feel that 'all women' need a good woman/bad woman model, suggests, in my view, that there is a continuing perception of the weak woman in need of guidance prevailing in Church thinking. The title 'Apostle of the Apostles' is therefore quite meaningless when its implications are not open to discussion.

On 15 August 2016, the Feast of the Assumption, Pope Francis instituted the 'Dicastery for the Laity, the Family and Life', which is to include women. A dicastery is a department of the Roman Curia, the administrative arm of the Holy See. Additionally, in September 2016 a symposium was convened to listen to the views of women theologians, canon lawyers, scripture scholars and specialists in other academic fields talking about the role of women in the Catholic Church and how they might contribute in the future. Cindy Wooden reports that the statement issued subsequently by the attending leaders of the Congregation for the Doctrine of the Faith stated: 'in addition to the formal presentations, participants "listened to interesting and moving testimonies" of the experiences of women in the Church, in theology, working in the Roman Curia or for bishops' conferences, in interreligious dialogue and ecumenism and in the field of Catholic charity'.[15] The word 'moving' conveys that women were listened to with a sympathetic ear, a useful means of procrastination. While much has been said by Pope Francis in terms of women's input to the Church in some shape or form, the clichés continue to be used, which in my view undermine the intent. It does seem that the men of the Church simply do not know what to do about women.

There is widespread resistance among conservative elements of the Church to this Pope's pastoral approach. Yet their voices have been included among the cardinals who advise Pope Francis, so that all opinions – liberal, conservative and moderate (aside from any woman's opinion, of course) – can be heard and included in discussions. At a presentation on his book, *Pope Francis Among the Wolves*, Marco Politi explained that the Pope, given that he celebrated his eightieth birthday in December 2016, is concerned that his reforms could be reversed before they have a chance to take hold.[16] The 2016 Year of Mercy was a call to the people of the Church to be merciful towards others, as the Pope has repeatedly said that he cannot 'open doors' by himself. While a pastoral approach from the papacy is to be welcomed, as is the realisation that women are a central part of the Christian story, the door to ordination remains firmly shut.

CONCLUSION

There is no doubt that the official Church is deeply uneasy when it comes to the question of the role of women in the Church. Yet, as we have seen throughout this exploration, women were central to Jesus' mission, and not merely on the periphery. This is why the early Christian movement appointed both men and women, married or single, as administrative and ministerial leaders. However, Church luminaries could not accept this. Nor could they accept that an ordinary woman, even when chosen by God, could be the mother of Jesus. Thus they took on the task of attributing an unnecessary designation of perpetual purity to Mary. They also turned their attention to Mary Magdalene, and were prepared to harm her reputation and legacy to suit their worldview. The fact that Christian men were willing to do such damage to Jesus' much-loved companion, who happened to be a woman, indicates the lengths to which the men of the institutional Church are prepared to go to maintain their men-only enclave. This is also demonstrated by the centuries-long campaigns of persecution, crusades and witch-hunts, which were a determined effort to eliminate dissent and served to both exclude and silence women from active participation in their Church. Coupled with the enforcement of a celibate clergy, achieved at the expense of women, the elimination of the feminine was achieved.

One of the reasons for undertaking this exploration was

because I wanted to find out why the Catholic Church is so deeply opposed to the idea of women in ministry. How can the Church, given the lack of evidence, justify its absolute conviction that not ordaining women as priests is part of God's plan for it? Given that there is no definitive prohibition in the scriptures about women ministering in the Church, it is difficult to understand why due consideration and discussion of women in ministry is forbidden. Rather, all focus has been centred on the maleness of the twelve apostles as well as the assumption that they, in turn, deliberately and specifically chose males, in the context of a permanent office, to succeed them, despite the lack of evidence for this teaching. We have seen, therefore, that the thinking came from the cultural milieu and the eventual infiltration of Roman law and culture, as promulgated by the Fathers of the Church, into the Latin Church, rather than from any real Christian tradition. Also evident is the decisiveness of Rome in the bid to establish a hierarchical structure and a measure of uniformity throughout the widely scattered Christian groups. Moreover, the bid by Rome for supremacy over all other cities is rather distasteful and, given the unlikelihood of Peter serving as Bishop of Rome, unwarranted.

One of the main points to be taken from our explorations of the early centuries of the Christian movement is the lack of coherence, structure and ritual as well as uniformity of thought. Not only are there differences in the canonical texts themselves, but the Gnostic texts point to the remarkable array of views about Jesus that were in circulation for a considerable period of time after his death. It is no surprise, therefore, that many of the teachings we have adopted as gospel, to coin a suitable phrase, are clearly influenced by prevailing cultural trends, or by the writings of Church Fathers, who were, in turn, presenting their interpretations of the gospels. The early Christian movement had to evolve so as to adapt and engage with the various environments in which Christian communities were established. By having recourse to Tradition, the gap between the early Church and the modern form can be bridged to provide a loose link of sorts between contradictory stances and conflicting evidence.

You may ask why it matters to raise such issues about a deeply flawed Church that does not see me, a woman, as being spiritually equal to a man. It matters because although the Church may now appear to be marginalised in the West, that is not the case in Africa, Asia and Latin America. It matters too because so many organised religions hold similar views about women's inferiority, a perception that has blighted the lives of women for centuries. It matters because ideas about the divine are linked to the status of women. Religion is supposed to be a force for good in society, yet one of the most important human rights issues today is the mistreatment and abuse of women and girls around the world. The World Health Organization reported in 2013 that one in three women will experience physical and/or sexual violence during their lifetime. Such commonplace abuse is reinforced by worldviews, both religious and cultural, that position women as secondary, inferior and spiritually incomplete. There is no question in my mind that inherited religious beliefs are highly influential in terms of cultural worldviews on women's positions and roles in society, especially when the scriptures and other sacred texts are used to support sexist and misogynist views. In short, the connection between the ideas Christians and followers of other religions have been taught about the divine, and the actual status of women cannot be underestimated. As long as world religions, supposedly founded on the edicts of love and human dignity, perpetuate the view that women are inferior, it is difficult to see how this situation can be reversed.

I also wanted to understand why the mere idea of women priests sends the Vatican into such a tailspin. The zealousness with which any discussion of women in priestly ministry has been suppressed can leave no doubt as to how deeply distasteful the idea is to the institutional Church. The sense of fear, and I use that word deliberately, emanating from the institutional Church on the issue of actual, as opposed to ideological, equality between the sexes, as witnessed by its defensive actions in relation to any discussion of women's roles in the Church, is difficult for present-day women to fathom. Women may have broken through the 'glass ceiling' in business, but to use Canon Ginnie Kennerley's phrase, we have yet to come anywhere close to breaking through the 'stained glass ceiling'.[1]

I also have some thoughts for my male readers. Have you ever considered what it might be like to be a woman in the Catholic Church? Bear in mind that women have to adjust to hearing everything from a male point of view when in church. How would you feel about being completely excluded from serving in your Church because of your gender? How would you feel about decisions and judgements being made about how you live your life without any consultation with you? How would you feel about being taught by your Church that you are spiritually inferior and do not have the same access to God because you do not resemble him physically? Indeed, how would you feel about the idea that God is a different gender from you?

What I can say at the end of my journey, is that, in my view, the scriptures are clear about the value of all in the eyes of Christ Jesus, in contrast to the implicit and frequently explicit Roman Catholic Church worldview that appears to pride itself on modes of distinctiveness. What I can also say is that a lack of certainty about what Jesus meant by everything he said and did, given the circumstances in which his story has been transcribed, does not, in my view, undermine the faith. However, as it stands, I can also say that in the current model of the male-centred and male-focused institutional Roman Catholic Church, there is no place for me.

So where do we go from here? In my view, it seems clear that women need no longer subscribe to Vatican views on their 'place', because these views stem from deeply flawed foundations. As Sue Monk Kidd, who underwent a similar experience of the realisation of the denial of the divine feminine in her faith system, writes in *The Dance of the Dissident Daughter*: 'Until a woman is willing to set aside her unquestioned loyalty and look critically at the tradition and convention of her faith, her awakening will never fully emerge.'[2] It seems to me that the most important step forward is to ensure that women are fully aware that the scriptures confirm they are created in the image and likeness of God, who is male and female, or beyond gender; that they are spiritual beings; and that the Holy Spirit does communicate with and inspire them. Furthermore, there is nothing inherently inferior, negative or 'sinful' about women as a gender category. These are labels imposed on women by a particular cultural mind-set.

While ordinary life has to a large extent dispensed with such labelling, in that awareness of the issue of sexism is slowly beginning to be acknowledged and addressed, the Church continues to subscribe to the thinking of long-gone centuries. That is no longer acceptable. Another difficulty I have is with the diametrically opposed edicts of, on the one hand, placing responsibility for the perpetuation of the faith on Catholic women, and on the other, limiting that responsibility, as well as insisting on the complete exclusion of women's voices from decision-making in the Church. That too is no longer acceptable. Until the Church acknowledges that its views on women are rooted in misogynistic and sexist mind-sets, and indeed that they need to ask women's pardon for the fundamental wrongs perpetuated on them as a result of centuries of sexist and misogynistic teachings in the past, any future remarks made by the institutional Church regarding women's roles are meaningless.

To uphold a decision, one has to have a reasonable argument, which the Church, in my view, has been unable to provide. From my perspective, and having explored the history behind the gospels, encyclicals and edicts, no reasonable argument exists against the ordination of women. My question to readers, then, is: given the abundance of material available to support the fact of women in ministry and women's active participation in the running of the early Church, as well as the large body of material analysing the reasoning and theology in the Vatican documents on the topic, do you think the exclusion of women from ministry is based on theological or sexist grounds?

As we have seen, John Paul II revisited the topic of female ordination on many occasions 'in order that all doubt may be removed'.[3] In this exploration, I have attempted to cast doubt on the absolutes in relation to the teachings and beliefs about women. The Catholic Church is absolutely sure that women cannot be in ministry because of their gender. My sentiment to my women readers at the end of this exploration is therefore similar to that spoken by Father Hugh at the end of the film *Ryan's Daughter*. As Rosie leaves her hometown with her husband, Charles, on the discovery of her affair with a British officer, Father Hugh, when bidding goodbye to Charles, tells him that if he and Rosie think they would be better off splitting up, he doubts it is the right decision. To use his words to them, I say the same about the 'certainties' we have been given for thousands of years about women's nature, secondary status and spiritual inferiority: 'That's my gift to you – that doubt!'[4]

ENDNOTES

The Major Eras of Christianity

1 Taken from Hans Küng, *Can We Save the Catholic Church? We Can Save the Catholic Church!* (London, William Collins, 2013).

Introduction

1 John Paul II, 'Introductory Letter', *Catechism of the Catholic Church* (Dublin, Veritas, 1994), p. 5.

1 The Early Christian Movement

1 I am indebted to the following books for this chapter: Averil Cameron, *The Later Roman Empire, AD 284–430* (London, Fontana Press, 1993); Mark Humphries, *Early Christianity* (London and New York, Routledge, 2006); Elaine Pagels, *The Gnostic Gospels* ([New York, Random House, 1979] London, Phoenix, 2006) and L. Michael White, *From Jesus to Christianity* (New York, HarperOne, 2004).

2 Humphries (2006), p. 103.

3 Pagels (2006), p. 112.

4 White (2004), p. 279.

5 Humphries (2006), p. 100.

6 White (2004), p. 95.

7 Thomas Moore, 'Introduction', *Writing in the Sand: Jesus, Spirituality and the Soul of the Gospels* (Alexandria, NSW, Hay House, 2009), p. xx.

8 The *Codex Iuris Canonici* is an ecclesiastical legal code consolidated as the Code of Canon Law in 1917 and revised in 1983. This is the official body of laws by which the Catholic Church is governed.

9   John Wijngaards, *The Ordination of Women in the Catholic Church: Unmasking a Cuckoo's Egg Tradition* (London, Darton, Longman & Todd, 2001), p. 97.

10 Cameron (1993), pp. 47, 56.

11 *Ibid.*, p. 77.

2   **No Women Allowed**

1   *Catechism of the Catholic Church* (Dublin, Veritas, 1994), para. 880.

2   The reasons, which I have summarised here, are enunciated more elaborately in John Paul II's Apostolic Letter, *On Reserving Priestly Ordination to Men Alone: Ordinatio Sacerdotalis* (22 May 1994).

3   *Catechism* (1994), para. 1577.

4   *Ibid.*, para. 611.

5   John Paul II (1994).

6   *Catechism* (1994), para. 77.

7   John Paul II (1994).

8   The references included here refer to the letters of Timothy and Titus, letters that in the past were attributed to Paul.

9   John Paul II (1994).

10 *Catechism* (1994) para. 77.

11 *Ibid.*, para. 78.

12 *Ibid.*, para. 860.

13 *Ibid.*

14 *Ibid.*

15 See also Mark 8.34; Matthew 8.18–22, 10.37–39, 16.24–28; Luke 9.57–62, 14.25–27, 17.33; John 12.25.

16 Küng (2013), p. 311.

17 *Catechism* (1994), para. 862.

18 *Ibid.*, para. 641.

19 *Ibid.*, para. 860.

20 Pagels (2006), pp. 36–8.

21 Quoted in *ibid.*, p. 69.

22 *Ibid.*, p. 41.

23 *Ibid.*

24 *Catholic Dictionary,* revised edition (Huntington, Our Sunday Visitor, 2002), p. 135.

25 Peter De Rosa, *Vicars of Christ: The Dark Side of the Papacy* (London, Corgi Books, 1989), p. 19. De Rosa is a former Dean of Theology at Corpus Christi in London, and left the priesthood in 1970.

26 Humphries (2006), p. 154.

27 *Ibid.*, p. 155.

28 Küng (2013), p. 103.

29 *Catechism* (1994), para. 882.

3 All About the Man

1 John Paul II (1994).

2 Paul VI, *Dogmatic Constitution on Divine Revelation: Dei Verbum* (18 November 1965).

3 *Ibid.*

4 *Ibid.*

5 *Ibid.*

6 *Acta Apostolicae Sedis* 68 (1976), pp. 599–604.

7 Pontifical Biblical Commission, 'Can Women Be Priests?', *Origins* 6 (1 July 1976), pp. 92–6.

8 Congregation for the Doctrine of the Faith, *Declaration on the Question of Admission of Women to the Ministerial Priesthood: Inter Insigniores* (15 October 1976).

9 For a detailed analysis and discussion of the studies and documents produced in the 1970s on women's role in religious structures, see Phyllis Zagano, *Holy Saturday: An Argument for the Restoration of the Female Diaconate in the Catholic Church* (New York, Crossroad Publishing Company, 2000), pp. 42–63.

10 The first woman deacon, Katherine Poulton, was ordained in the Church of Ireland in 1987. It was ten years after the legislation

was drafted before the ordination of women took place in the UK. On 12 March 1994 thirty-two women were ordained in Bristol Cathedral in England. The first female bishop in Ireland and the UK, Pat Storey, Bishop of Meath and Kildare, was appointed in 2013. For a personal account of the development of women's ordained ministry in the Church of Ireland, see Ginnie Kennerley, *Embracing Women: Making History in the Church of Ireland* (Dublin, Columba Press, 2008).

11 Mary T. Malone, *Women and Christianity. Vol. 3: From the Reformation to the 21st Century* (Dublin, Columba Press, 2003), p. 229.

12 *Ibid.*, p. 231.

13 Quoted in *ibid.*, p. 232.

14 *Ibid.*

15 John Paul II, *On the Dignity and Vocation of Women on the Occasion of the Marian Year: Mulieris Dignitatem* (15 August 1988), Apostolic Letter.

16 John Paul II (1994).

17 *Ibid.*

18 *Ibid.*

19 *Ibid.*

20 Wijngaards (2001), p. 37.

21 John Paul II (1994).

22 Congregation for the Doctrine of the Faith, *Responsum ad Propositum Dubium Concerning the Teaching contained in "Ordinatio Sacerdotalis"* (28 October 1995).

23 John Paul II, *Ad Tuendam Fidem* (To Defend the Faith), by which certain norms are inserted into the *Code of Canon Law* and into the *Code of Canons of the Eastern Churches* (18 May 1998), Apostolic Letter.

24 Congregation for the Doctrine of the Faith, *Letter to the Bishops of the Catholic Church on the Collaboration of Men and Women in the Church and in the World* (31 May 2004).

25 *Ibid.*

26 John Paul II (1988).

27 Congregation for the Doctrine of the Faith, *A brief introduction to the modifications made in the Normae de gravioribus delictis, reserved to the Congregation for the Doctrine of the Faith* (21 May 2010).

28 Fiona Govan, 'Church rejects women bishops', *The Irish Times*, 20 November 2012, www.irishtimes.com/newspaper/breaking/2012/1120/breaking54.html (accessed 24 November 2012).

29 Francis I, *Evangelii Gaudium* (The Joy of the Gospel), *Apostolic Exhortation on the Proclamation of the Gospel in Today's World* (24 November 2013).

30 See United States Catholic Conference, *John Paul II on the Genius of Women* (Washington DC, United States Catholic Conference Publication, 1997).

31 Francis I (2013).

32 Patsy McGarry, 'Australian priest first to be excommunicated by Pope Francis', *The Irish Times*, 26 September 2013, http://www.irishtimes.com/news/social-affairs/religion-and-beliefs/australian-priest-first-to-be-excommunicated-by-pope-francis-1.1541165?page=2 (accessed 10 January 2014).

33 Paddy Agnew, 'Pope calls for church that "keeps the doors open"', *The Irish Times*, 20 September 2013, https://www.irishtimes.com/news/social-affairs/pope-calls-for-church-that-keeps-the-doors-open-1.1533828 (accessed 27 June 2017).

34 John Paul II (1994).

35 Congregation for the Doctrine of the Faith (1976).

36 *Catechism* (1994), para. 1549.

37 Congregation for the Doctrine of the Faith (1976).

38 Quoted in Wijngaards (2001), p. 101.

39 Congregation for the Doctrine of the Faith (1976).

40 John Paul II (1988).

41 *Ibid.*

42 Quoted in Wijngaards (2001), p. 119.

43 Tina Beattie, *New Catholic Feminism: Theology and Theory* (London and New York, Routledge, 2006), p. 132.

44 John Paul II (1988).

45 Pius XI, *On Christian Marriage: Casti Connubii* (31 December 1930), Encyclical.

46 Francis I (2013).

47 Gary Macy, *The Hidden History of Women's Ordination: Female Clergy in the Medieval West* (New York, Oxford University Press, 2008), p. 30.

48 *Ibid.*, p. 31.

49 *Ibid.*, pp. 108–9.

4   What About the Women?

1 *HarperCollins Study Bible*, revised edition (London, HarperCollins, 1993), p. 7.

2 Julian of Norwich, *Revelations of Divine Love*, trans. and intro. M. L. del Mastro (New York, Image Books, 1977), p. 173.

3 Quoted in Mary T. Malone, *Four Women Doctors of the Church* (Dublin, Veritas, 2015), p. 63.

4 For similar 'awakenings' about the perception of women in organised religion, see Alaa Murabit, 'What my religion really says about women' (TedWomen, filmed May 2015), https://www.ted.com/talks/alaa_murabit_what_my_religion_really_says_about_women; Chelsea Shields, 'How I'm working for change inside my church', Ted Fellows Retreat (filmed August 2015), https://www.ted.com/talks/chelsea_shields_how_i_m_working_for_change_inside_my_church.

On the role of scripture and the status of women, see Jimmy Carter, 'Why I believe the mistreatment of women is the number one human rights abuse' (TedWomen, filmed May 2015), https://www.ted.com/talks/jimmy_carter_why_i_believe_the_mistreatment_of_women_is_the_number_one_human_rights_abuse?language=en.

5   *The New Jerusalem Bible* (1985), http://www.catholic.org/bible/ (accessed 16 April 2013).

6   Quoted in Pagels (2006), p. 84.

7   Wilhelm Schneemelcher (ed.), *New Testament Apocrypha*, Vol. 2 (Cambridge, James Clarke/Louisville, Kentucky, Westminster & John Knox Press, 1992).

8   *Ibid.*, p. 267.

9   *Ibid.*, p. 269.

10 Mary T. Malone, *Women and Christianity. Vol. 1: The First Thousand Years* (Dublin, Columba Press, 2000), p. 93.

11 See www.womenpriests.org (accessed 15 January 2014).

5   The Fall of Women in the Catholic Church

1   Quoted in Marina Warner, *Alone of All Her Sex: The Myth and Cult of the Virgin Mary* (London, Vintage, 2000), p. 27.

2   See Esther Harding, *Woman's Mysteries: Ancient and Modern* (New York, Harper & Row, 1971).

3   Quoted in Uta Ranke-Heinemann, *Eunuchs for Heaven: The Catholic Church and Sexuality*, trans. John Brownjohn ([Hamburg, Heyne Verlag, 1988] London, Andre Deutsch, 1990), p. 309.

4   John Paul II, *The Mother of the Redeemer: Redemptoris Mater* (25 March 1987), Encyclical.

5   Susan Haskins, *Mary Magdalen: Myth and Metaphor* (London, Pimlico, 2005). Haskins' remarkable book explores 2,000 years of literature, art and history to examine the depiction of Mary Magdalene and reappraise her significance in the Christian story.

6   *Ibid.*, p. 93.

7   *Ibid.*, p. 152.

8   *Ibid.*, pp. 96–7.

9   *Ibid.*, p. 388.

10 Mary T. Malone, *The Elephant in the Church: A Woman's Tract for Our Times* (Dublin, Columba Press, 2014), p. 27.

11 Quoted in Wijngaards (2001), p. 137.

6 The Celibate Man Versus the Carnal Woman

1 *Catechism* (1994), para. 1579.

2 Karen Armstrong, *The Gospel According to Woman: Christianity's Creation of the Sex War in the West* (London, Elm Tree Books, 1986), p. 4.

3 Ranke-Heinemann (1990), pp. 22–4.

4 *Ibid.*, p. 62.

5 *Ibid.*, p. 105.

6 *Ibid.*, pp. 28–9.

7 Quoted in Wijngaards (2001), p. 102.

8 *Ibid.*

9 In Aeschylus' *Orestia*, for example, Apollo pronounces that it is less serious for Orestes to have killed his mother than his father, as she is merely the carrier of the seed: 'The mother is no parent of that which is called her child, but only nurse of the new-planted seed that grows. The parent is he who mounts.' Aeschylus, *Oresteia: Agamemnon, The Libation Bearers, The Eumenides*, editors David Grene and Richmond Lattimore, trans. Richmond Lattimore (Chicago/London, University of Chicago Press, 1953), p. 158. The remnants of this belief lingered until the discovery of the ovum in 1827 by E. von Baer (Ranke-Heinemann (1990) p. 164).

10 Armstrong (1986), pp. 37–8.

11 Ranke-Heinemann (1990), p. 120.

12 *Ibid.*, p. 121.

13 *Ibid.*, pp. 183–5.

14 Armstrong (1986), p. 260.

15 *Ibid.*, p. 264.

16 *Ibid.*, pp. 279–80.

17 De Rosa (1989), p. 583.

18 Marie Keenan, *Child Sexual Abuse and the Catholic Church: Gender, Power, and Organizational Culture* (New York, Oxford University Press, 2012), p. 61.

19 *Catechism* (1994), paras 2332–2364.

20 Keenan (2012), p. 25.

21 Malone (2003), p. 30.

22 Mary T. Malone, *Women and Christianity. Vol. 2: The Medieval Period AD 1000–1500* (Dublin, Columba Press, 2001), pp. 203–7.

7 Dilemmas and Contradictions

1 *Concise Oxford English Dictionary*, twelfth edition (Oxford, Oxford University Press, 2011), p. 1529.

2 *Catechism* (1994), para. 83.

3 *Ibid.*, paras 80–2.

4 De Rosa (1989), p. 187.

5 Quoted in Wijngaards (2001), p. 185, note 1.

6 *Catechism* (1994), para. 1267.

7 *Ibid.*, para. 1121.

8 Armstrong (1986), p. 301.

9 Douglas Dalby, 'Priest is planning to defy the Vatican's orders to stay quiet', *The New York Times*, 19 January 2013, https://mobile.nytimes.com/2013/01/20/world/europe/priest-is-planning-to-defy-vaticans-orders-to-stasy-quiet.html (accessed 8 March 2013).

10 See Fr Bourgeois' webpage: 'My Journey from Silence to Solidarity', http://www.roybourgeoisjourney.org/ (accessed 26 June 2017).

11 Francis I (2013).

12 McGarry, *The Irish Times*, 26 September 2013.

13 Congregation for Divine Worship and the Discipline of the Sacraments, 'Apostle of the Apostles' (3 June 2016).

14 *Ibid.*

15 Cindy Wooden, 'Doctrinal Congregation convokes meeting on role of women in the church', *National Catholic Reporter*, 29 September 2016, https://www.ncronline.org/news/vatican/doctrinal-congregation-convokes-meeting-role-women-church (accessed 19 October 2016).

16 Marco Politi, presentation on his book, *Pope Francis Among the Wolves: The Inside Story of a Revolution*, trans. William McCuaig

(New York, Columbia University Press, 2015), delivered at Trinity Chapel, Trinity College Dublin, 15 October 2016.

Conclusion

1 Kennerley (2008), p. 16.

2 Sue Monk Kidd, *The Dance of the Dissident Daughter: A Woman's Journey from Christian Tradition to the Sacred Feminine* (New York, HarperCollins, 1996), p. 59.

3 John Paul II (1994).

4 *Ryan's Daughter*, Dir. David Lean (Metro-Goldwyn-Mayer, 1970).

BIBLIOGRAPHY

Books, Journals and Newspaper Articles

Aeschylus, *Oresteia: Agamemnon, The Libation Bearers, The Eumenides*, editors David Grene and Richmond Lattimore, trans. Richmond Lattimore (Chicago/London, University of Chicago Press, 1953)

Agnew, Paddy, 'Pope calls for church that "keeps the doors open"', *The Irish Times*, 20 September 2013, https://www.irishtimes.com/news/social-affairs/pope-calls-for-church-that-keeps-the-doors-open-1.1533828 (accessed 27 June 2017)

Armstrong, Karen, *The Gospel According to Woman: Christianity's Creation of the Sex War in the West* (London, Elm Tree Books, 1986)

Beattie, Tina, *New Catholic Feminism: Theology and Theory* (London/New York, Routledge, 2006)

Cameron, Averil, *The Later Roman Empire, AD 284–430* (London, Fontana Press, 1993)

Dalby, Douglas, 'Priest is planning to defy the Vatican's orders to stay quiet', *The New York Times*, 19 January 2013, https://mobile.nytimes.com/2013/01/20/world/europe/priest-is-planning-to-defy-vaticans-orders-to-stay-quiet.html (accessed 8 March 2013)

De Rosa, Peter, *Vicars of Christ: The Dark Side of the Papacy* (London, Corgi Books, 1989)

Flannery, Tony, *A Question of Conscience* (Dublin, Londubh Books, 2013)

Govan, Fiona, 'Church rejects women bishops', *The Irish Times*, 20 November 2012, www.irishtimes.com/newspaper/breaking/2012/1120/breaking54.html (accessed 24 November 2012)

Harding, Esther, *Woman's Mysteries: Ancient and Modern* (New York, Harper & Row, 1971)

Haskins, Susan, *Mary Magdalen: Myth and Metaphor* (London, Pimlico, 2005)

Humphries, Mark, *Early Christianity* (London and New York, Routledge, 2006)

Julian of Norwich, *Revelations of Divine Love*, trans. and intro. M. L. del Mastro (New York, Image Books, 1977)

Keenan, Marie, *Child Sexual Abuse and the Catholic Church: Gender, Power, and Organizational Culture* (New York, Oxford University Press, 2012)

Kennerley, Ginnie, *Embracing Women: Making History in the Church of Ireland* (Dublin, Columba Press, 2008)

Kramer, Heinrich and James Sprenger, *The Malleus Maleficarum of Heinrich Kramer and James Sprenger*, trans. Montague Summers (London, 1928) (An unabridged online version of the 1928 edition is available at https://archive.org/details/TheMalleusMaleficarum)

Küng, Hans, *Can We Save the Catholic Church? We Can Save the Catholic Church!* (London, William Collins, 2013)

Machiavelli, Niccolò, *The Prince*, trans. George Anthony Bull. Penguin Classics Series (New York/London, Penguin Books, 1999)

Macy, Gary, *The Hidden History of Women's Ordination: Female Clergy in the Medieval West* (New York, Oxford University Press, 2008)

Malone, Mary T., *Women & Christianity: Vol. 1: The First Thousand Years* (Dublin, Columba Press, 2000)

Malone, Mary T., *Women & Christianity: Vol. 2: The Medieval Period, AD 1000–1500* (Dublin, Columba Press, 2001)

Malone, Mary T., *Women & Christianity: Vol. 3: From the Reformation to the 21st Century* (Dublin, Columba Press, 2003)

Malone, Mary T., *The Elephant in the Church: A Woman's Tract for Our Times* (Dublin, Columba Press, 2014)

Malone, Mary T., *Four Women Doctors of the Church* (Dublin, Veritas, 2015)

McAleese, Mary, *Reconciled Being: Love in Chaos* (London, Arthur James, 1997)

McGarry, Patsy, 'Australian priest first to be excommunicated by Pope Francis', *The Irish Times*, 26 September 2013, http://www.irishtimes.

com/news/social-affairs/religion-and-beliefs/australian-priest-first-to-be-excommunicated-by-pope-francis-1.1541165?page=2 (accessed 10 January 2014)

Monk Kidd, Sue, *The Dance of the Dissident Daughter: A Woman's Journey from Christian Tradition to the Sacred Feminine* (New York, HarperCollins, 1996)

Moore, Thomas, *Writing in the Sand: Jesus, Spirituality and the Soul of the Gospels* (Alexandria, NSW, Hay House, 2009)

Pagels, Elaine, *The Gnostic Gospels* ([New York, Random House, 1979] London, Phoenix, 2006)

Politi, Marco, *Pope Francis Among the Wolves: The Inside Story of a Revolution*, trans. William McCuaig (New York, Columbia University Press, 2015)

Ranke-Heinemann, Uta, *Eunuchs for Heaven: The Catholic Church and Sexuality*, trans. John Brownjohn ([Hamburg, Heyne Verlag, 1988, in German] London, Andre Deutsch, 1990)

Schneemelcher, Wilhelm (ed.), *New Testament Apocrypha*, Vol. 2 (Cambridge, James Clarke/Louisville, Kentucky, Westminster & John Knox Press, 1992)

United States Catholic Conference, *John Paul II on the Genius of Women* (Washington, DC, United States Catholic Conference Publication, 1997)

Warner, Marina, *Alone of All Her Sex: The Myth and Cult of the Virgin Mary* (London, Vintage, 2000)

White, L. Michael, *From Jesus to Christianity* (New York, HarperOne, 2004)

Wijngaards, John, *The Ordination of Women in the Catholic Church: Unmasking a Cuckoo's Egg Tradition* (London, Darton, Longman & Todd, 2001)

Wooden, Cindy, 'Doctrinal Congregation convokes meeting on role of women in the church', *National Catholic Reporter*, 29 September 2016, https://www.ncronline.org/news/vatican/doctrinal-congregation-convokes-meeting-role-women-church (accessed 19 October 2016)

Zagano, Phyllis, *Holy Saturday: An Argument for the Restoration of the Female Diaconate in the Catholic Church* (New York, Crossroad Publishing Company, 2000)

Other Sources

Association of Catholic Priests (ACP), http://www.associationof-catholicpriests.ie/

Bourgeois, Roy, 'My Journey from Silence to Solidarity', http://www.roybourgeoisjourney.org/ (accessed 26 June 2017)

Carter, Jimmy, 'Why I believe the mistreatment of women is the number one human rights abuse' (TedWomen, filmed May 2015), https://www.ted.com/talks/jimmy_carter_why_i_believe_the_mistreatment_of_women_is_the_number_one_human_rights_abuse?language=en

Murabit, Alaa, 'What my religion really says about women' (Ted-Women, filmed May 2015), https://www.ted.com/talks/alaa_murabit_what_my_religion_really_says_about_women

Ryan's Daughter, Dir. David Lean (Metro-Goldwyn-Mayer, 1970)

Shields, Chelsea, 'How I'm working for change inside my church', Ted Fellows Retreat (filmed August 2015), https://www.ted.com/talks/chelsea_shields_how_i_m_working_for_change_inside_my_church

Wijngaards Institute for Catholic Research, http://www.women-priests.org/

Would You Believe, RTÉ One, 17 January 2011, documentary (presenter: Mick Peelo)

Reference Books/Sources

Catechism of the Catholic Church (Dublin, Veritas, 1994)

Catholic Dictionary, revised edition (Huntington, Our Sunday Visitor, 2002)

Concise Oxford English Dictionary, twelfth edition (Oxford, Oxford University Press, 2011)

HarperCollins Study Bible, revised edition (London, HarperCollins, 1993)

Holy Bible: The Douay–Rheims Translation, http://www.catholicdoors.com/bible/ (accessed 15 June 2013)

New Jerusalem Bible, The, http://www.catholic.org/bible/ (accessed 15 June 2013)

Vatican Sources and Documents (all available at www.Vatican.va, except 'Can Women be Priests?')

Acta Apostolicae Sedis (*AAS*) 68 (1976)

Congregation for Divine Worship and the Discipline of the Sacraments, 'Apostle of the Apostles' (3 June 2016)

Congregation for the Doctrine of the Faith, *Declaration on the Question of Admission of Women to the Ministerial Priesthood: Inter Insigniores* (15 October 1976)

Congregation for the Doctrine of the Faith, *Responsum ad Propositum Dubium Concerning the Teaching contained in "Ordinatio Sacerdotalis"* (28 October 1995)

Congregation for the Doctrine of the Faith, *Letter to the Bishops of the Catholic Church on the Collaboration of Men and Women in the Church and in the World* (31 May 2004)

Congregation for the Doctrine of the Faith, *A brief introduction to the modifications made in the Normae de gravioribus delictis, reserved to the Congregation for the Doctrine of the Faith* (21 May 2010)

Congregation for the Doctrine of the Faith, *Decree of Erection of the Personal Ordinariate of Our Lady of Walsingham* (15 January 2011)

Francis I, *Evangelii Gaudium* (The Joy of the Gospel), *Apostolic Exhortation on the Proclamation of the Gospel in Today's World* (24 November 2013)

John Paul II, *The Mother of the Redeemer: Redemptoris Mater* (25 March 1987), Encyclical

John Paul II, *On the Dignity and Vocation of Women on the Occasion of the Marian Year: Mulieris Dignitatem* (15 August 1988), Apostolic Letter

John Paul II, *On Reserving Priestly Ordination to Men Alone: Ordinatio Sacerdotalis* (22 May 1994), Apostolic Letter to the Bishops of the Catholic Church

John Paul II, *Ad Tuendam Fidem* (To Defend the Faith), by which certain norms are inserted into the *Code of Canon Law* and into the *Code of Canons of the Eastern Churches* (18 May 1998), Apostolic Letter Moto Proprio

Paul VI, *Dogmatic Constitution on the Church: Lumen gentium* (21 November 1964), Second Vatican Council Document

Paul VI, *Dogmatic Constitution on Divine Revelation: Dei Verbum* (18 November 1965), Second Vatican Council Document

Pius XI, *On Christian Marriage*: *Casti Connubii* (31 December 1930), Encyclical

Pontifical Biblical Commission, 'Can Women Be Priests?', *Origins* 6 (1 July 1976)